RECIPES FOR A SONG

The Mendocino Women's Choir Cookbook

LOST
COAST
PRESS

Recipes for a Song
The Mendocino Women's Choir Cookbook
© 2011 Mendocino Women's Choir

Mendocino Women's Choir
155 Cypress Street
Fort Bragg, CA 95437
www.mendocinowomenschoir.org
(800) 773-7783

To order additional copies, please contact:

Lost Coast Press
155 Cypress Street
Fort Bragg, California 95437
(800) 773-7783
Fax: 707-964-9520
www.cypresshouse.com
Email: bookorders@cypresshouse.com

ISBN: 978-1-935448-14-3
Manufactured in the USA
2 4 6 8 0 7 5 3
Cover design and photographs by Chuck Hathaway
Book design by Alexandra Pierangeli
alex@demi-geekette.com
www.demi-geekette.com

Contributors are in Bell MT Italic; fractions are in Times New Roman. Body text is Portland LDO designed by Luke Owens; section heads are in Captain's Table by Roulette Studios; recipe names and other headings are in Mariah, designed with Fontographer in 1993. The sub-recipe names are in Halcyon, designed by L'Abécédarienne, in 2004 "with the helping hands and eyes of Mark Clarin."

The section illustration for Breakfast is the frontispiece ("Prinzessin Marie und Rosaurus") from the Project Gutenberg ebook of *Leben und Schicksale des Katers Rosaurus* by Amalie Winter.

To Our Moms

Table of Contents

Acknowledgments

Many thanks—

To our wonderful community, supportive local businesses, fans, and sister-singers. We wouldn't be us without you!

To Cheri Langlois, for allowing her email program to be overloaded with everyone's recipes, and who kept and ordered the master list, while gently nagging us about deadlines and details.

To Sal Glynn, for hours of copyediting, and more than a few entertaining editorial queries.

To Alexandra Pierangeli, for her lovely book design and layout.

To Chuck Hathaway of Mendocino Graphics, for his smashing cover design, along with organizing one of the funniest photo shoots.

To our indexers, Peter Brigaitis and Marie Nuchols, for without whom we couldn't find anything.

To Cypress House, for assistance in the book's production, sales, and distribution.

To McNaughton-Gunn, for donating their resources to create a beautifully printed book.

Introduction

Founded in 1992 by singer/composer Margy Crowningshield, singers Cynthia Frank and Sharon Hansen, and poet Karin Faulkner, the Mendocino Women's Choir has been together for almost twenty years. We're a feminist, progressive, loving, and sassy non-audition community choir. Over the years, the size of our choir has varied from 24 to 105 singers (yikes!), and our ages ranged from 14 to 80. We perform a variety of music, from Mozart to Bartok, Bulgarian folk music to doo-wop, Holly Near to Gregorian chant, and PDQ Bach to gospel.

We've performed for weddings, birthdays, and memorials, at sickbeds and parades, for environmental causes, museum dedications, and political fundraisers. We've had the pleasure of joining the Mendocino Music Festival Chorus for Beethoven's *Symphony No. 9 in D Minor*, the Brahms *Requiem*, Mozart's *Grand Mass in C Minor*, Stravinsky's *Symphony of Psalms*, Orff's *Carmina Burana*, and an evening of opera choruses.

Occasionally, we get to travel and sing outside of Mendocino County. We've had marvelous adventures singing at the Northern California Women's Choir Invitational, Northern California Women's Music Festival, West Coast A Cappella Summit, Carnegie Hall, the Chapel at Ground Zero, and the Northern California Women's Chorus Dinner Party Tour to Los Angeles.

As we've learned to combine vocal ingredients into a sonorous repast, as we learn the notes, rhythms, and dynamics, and explore the musical and emotional subtleties of each song, we blend each individual voice into the whole choir. Then we add a soupçon of riser choreography, dancers, and percussion. We garnish our performances with small ensembles and soloists. We've done much the same thing with this cookbook. Each choir member or supporter submitted recipes in her or his tonal range. Coming from our hearts and varied experience, each recipe has different rhythms and counterpoint—you are invited to add your own spicy rhythms or personal harmonies.

Funds from the sale of this cookbook will help provide scholarships for choir members who would not otherwise be able to sing with us in June 2012 when we travel to London to sing under the baton of Rollo Dilworth at Southwark and Canterbury cathedrals as part of the pre-Olympics celebrations. We will also present a benefit concert for a non-profit organization in London. And when we arrive at Stonehenge, our music will fill the air!

We hope you enjoy using this cookbook as much as we have enjoyed preparing it and performing for you.

Mendocino Women's Choir Cookbook editorial committee: Camille Ranker, Cheri Langlois, Cynthia Frank, Meadow, Myra Beals, Alexandra Pierangeli.

Visit us at www.mendocinowomenschoir.org

BREADS AND ROLLS

Best in Show Sweet Bread

Contributed by June Lemos

This is an old family recipe that I have altered over the years. It won Best in Show for baked goods at the Mendocino County Fair in 1990 and is regularly enjoyed by my family on holidays.

Yield: 2 loaves   **Prep: 1 hr, plus 2 hrs rising time**   **Baking: 35 min**

2 packages (4½ teaspoons) active dry yeast
⅓ cup water
1 medium russet potato, boiled
¼ cup milk
½ cup butter (1 stick), melted
¾ cup sugar
4 cups flour
3 eggs
1 teaspoon salt
2 teaspoons vanilla
2 teaspoons lemon extract
1 egg yolk, beaten
Sugar for sprinkling

In a mixing bowl, combine the yeast with the water and a pinch of sugar, and let sit for 10 minutes or until foamy. In another bowl, mash the boiled potato well and combine with the milk, butter, and sugar. Make sure the mixture is absolutely smooth and there are no lumps. Add the proofed yeast to the potato mixture and beat in half of the flour until well blended. Add the eggs, salt, vanilla, and lemon. Add more flour, half a cup at a time, to make soft dough. Knead on a lightly floured surface until smooth, shiny, and elastic.

Preheat the oven to 350°. Form dough into a ball and place in a greased bowl, turning to coat all sides. Cover bowl with a clean towel or plastic wrap and set in a warm, draft-free place until doubled, about two hours. Punch down, knead briefly, and let stand for 10 minutes. Divide dough in half and form 2 smooth balls. Place in the center of 2 greased 9-inch cake pans and let rise until doubled, about one hour. Beat the egg yolk with a little water and brush the mixture on the top of each loaf, and sprinkle lightly with sugar. Bake for 35 minutes. Remove loaves from oven and place on rack. Let cool completely before slicing.

Cottage Cheese Herb Bread

Contributed by Cynthia Frank

Yield: 2 loaves   **Prep: 2½ hrs**   **Baking: 40 - 50 min**

2 tablespoons yeast
½ cup warm milk
2 cups cottage cheese, creamed
½ teaspoon baking soda
3 tablespoons butter, melted, or olive oil
2 eggs, beaten
1½ teaspoons salt
⅔ cup fresh chives, finely chopped
4½ cups white flour or half whole wheat/half white flour
1 tablespoon olive oil

In a large mixing bowl, stir the yeast into milk. Add the cottage cheese, baking soda, butter, eggs, salt, and chives. Stir in the flour and mix well. Turn out the dough on a floured board. Knead until smooth and no longer sticky. Add more flour in small amounts if necessary.

Roll the dough into a ball, rub with oil, and place in a greased mixing bowl. Cover lightly and put in warm spot away from drafts for 1½ hours, or until double in size. Punch down the dough. Divide into two loaves and place seam-side down in greased loaf pans. Cover lightly and let rise in warm place away from drafts for 1 hour, or until double in size. Preheat oven to 350° and bake for 40 to 50 minutes. Remove loaves from oven and place on rack. Let cool completely before slicing.

Cinnamon Rolls

Contributed by Robert Goleman

As a child, a favorite treat was my mother's cinnamon rolls. Waiting was agony. The smell, even while rising, kept my taste buds on edge knowing that it would be hours before they were ready to eat. She made them rarely and when one batch was gone, I'd begin dreaming of the next. This recipe can be made by hand, or started in a bread machine and finished by hand. (I always make the dough the night before and allow it to rise the first time in the refrigerator, then roll out the dough out and finish the process in the morning. Cold dough is much easier to handle and the final ingredients stay in place.)

Yield: 8 large rolls　　　**Prep: 1 hr (3½ hrs, start to finish)**　　　**Baking: 35 - 45 min**

1¼ cups milk
2 tablespoons dried dairy whey or powdered milk
2 tablespoons sugar
2 tablespoons unsalted butter
3 teaspoons active dry yeast or 2 teaspoons fast rising yeast
3¼ cups white bread flour
1 teaspoon salt
1 teaspoon ground coriander
½ tablespoon lemon zest
1 egg, well beaten
⅓ cup unsalted butter, melted
½ cup dark brown sugar
1½ tablespoons ground cinnamon
½ cup raisins or currants *(optional)*
1 cup walnuts or pecans, chopped *(optional)*

In a small saucepan, combine the milk, whey, sugar, and butter. Place over low heat and bring to a simmer, stirring constantly. Remove from the heat and let cool to 80°. Add the yeast and let stand for 10 minutes, or until bubbly. In a large mixing bowl, stir together the flour, salt, coriander, and lemon zest. Add the yeast mixture to the flour mixture, along with the egg. Mix well.

For making the dough using a bread machine: Combine all the ingredients except the last five. Process and allow dough to go through the first rise.

5

On a well-floured surface, knead the dough for about 10 minutes until it is soft, silken, and elastic. Place the dough in a large, greased bowl, turning the dough to grease both sides. Cover the bowl with plastic wrap. In a warm area away from drafts, let the dough rise until it has doubled in bulk (1 to 1½ hours).

Punch the dough down. On a well-floured surface, roll the dough into a half-inch thick rectangle (12 x 20 in), aiding the process by pulling and shaping with the fingers. Brush the dough liberally with the melted butter. Sprinkle on the brown sugar and then cover generously, but not too heavily, with the cinnamon. Sprinkle on the currants and nuts.

Starting from a short end, loosely roll up the dough to form a log. Cut the roll into eight even-sized slices. Carefully place the slices on a greased baking sheet, sliced sides up and down. Space the rolls about 2 inches apart. Cover the rolls with a thin dishtowel and let rise until they double in bulk (30 minutes to 1 hour).

Preheat the oven to 350°. Uncover the rolls and place in a baking pan. Cover with foil to prevent over-browning and bake for 35 to 45 minutes. Cool in the pan on a wire rack. Before the cinnamon rolls cool completely, drizzle with vanilla icing.

Vanilla Icing

1 cup powdered confectioner's sugar
4 tablespoons (½ stick) unsalted butter, melted
2 tablespoons half and half or cream
1 teaspoon vanilla extract or seeds scraped from half a vanilla bean

In a mixing bowl, combine all the ingredients until very smooth. Add more half and half if necessary to bring the icing to a barely pourable yet smooth consistency.

Gingerbread

Contributed by Cynthia Frank

Yield: 1 loaf　　　　　　**Prep: 10 min**　　　　　　**Baking: 50 - 60 min**

2½ cups white flour or half whole wheat/half white flour
3 teaspoons powdered ginger
2 teaspoons dry mustard
1½ teaspoons baking soda
1 teaspoon cinnamon
pinch of salt
½ cup butter (1 stick), melted
¼ cup honey
1 egg
⅔ cup applesauce
1 cup molasses
1 cup hot water (not boiling)

Preheat oven to 350°. In mixing bowl, combine the flour, ginger, mustard, baking soda, and cinnamon. In a separate bowl, combine the remaining ingredients in order. Stir the dry ingredients into butter/honey mixture and pour into greased 8 x 11 pan (or two small loaf pans). Bake for 50 to 60 minutes or until toothpick comes out clean. Let pan cool and spread loaf with icing. Great served with sliced mangoes.

Icing

2¾ cups powdered sugar, sifted
3 tablespoons water
2 teaspoons pure vanilla extract

In a mixing bowl, combine the ingredients until very smooth. Add more water if necessary to bring the icing to a spreadable consistency. Dust with roasted coconut flakes.

Sally's Gluten-Free Seed and Nut Bread

Contributed by Sally Fletcher

This hearty and healthy basic gluten-free bread recipe makes for great toast. You can vary the seed and nut ingredients to create your own favorite types of breads.

Yield: 1 loaf   **Prep: 1½ hrs, including rising**   **Baking: 50 min**

½ cup brown rice flour
½ cup sorghum flour
¼ cup quinoa flour
½ cup sweet or white rice flour
1 cup tapioca flour
   (If using pre-mixed gluten-free flours, use 3¼ cups total flour.)
½ cup arrowroot starch
⅓ cup almonds or walnuts, ground until still a bit chunky
2½ teaspoons guar gum or 2 teaspoons xanthan gum
2 tablespoons granulated sugar
1 teaspoon gluten-free dough conditioner *(optional)*
1 teaspoon salt
⅓ teaspoon cinnamon
½ cup water
1 package (2¼ teaspoons) active dry yeast
1 teaspoon granulated sugar
2 large egg whites
¾ cup warm water
2 tablespoons toasted sesame seeds or poppy seeds
¼ cup Earth Balance or butter, melted

Preheat the oven to 170° and then turn off and open door part way. Make sure all ingredients are at room temperature. Lightly grease a 4 x 8 inch loaf pan (5 x 9 inch for a slightly lower loaf).

In the bowl of a stand mixer, use the paddle to sift together the dry ingredients except for the nuts and the yeast, and transfer to a mixing bowl. Heat water to 110°. In a small bowl or measuring cup, stir together yeast and one teaspoon of sugar.

Add the water to the yeast mixture and mix well. Let stand for 10 minutes, or until foamy on top.

While yeast is activating, put egg whites in mixer bowl and whisk well using paddle. Once the yeast is ready, add to the dry ingredients, along with the nuts, the egg whites, and Earth Balance. Add the warm water (reserving a little at first) and mix on low/medium until the right consistency is achieved. The dough should be like very stiff cake batter. Now beat the dough on medium/high for about 5 minutes. If you have added too much water add a little rice flour until you achieve the right dough consistency (if too stiff, add a little water).

Put the dough in prepared pan and use a large wetted spoon to smooth top and sprinkle on sesame seeds. Lightly pat down the seeds. Place in the oven cooled to 80 to 90° and let rise for 45 minutes with a light towel over the pan. About 10 minutes before the rising is finished, remove the pan from the oven and keep in a warm place. Preheat the oven to 350°. Bake the bread for 50 minutes or until internal temperature reaches 208°. Remove from pan immediately and cool on rack.

Persimmon Corn Bread

Contributed by Rachel Lahn

Serves: 6 to 8   **Prep: 30 min**   **Baking: 30 min**

1 cup cornmeal
¾ cup wheat or spelt flour
¼ cup polenta
1 tablespoon baking powder
1 teaspoon salt
¼ cup sugar, honey, or maple syrup
⅓ cup vegetable oil
2 eggs, beaten
1 cup milk
2 cups ripe persimmon pulp

Preheat the oven to 400°. In a mixing bowl, combine dry ingredients and mix well. Use a food processor to blend sugar, oil, eggs, milk, and persimmon pulp. Add the wet ingredients to the dry ingredients and mix well. Pour into well-oiled 8-inch pan. Bake for 30 minutes or until fork comes out clean.

BREAKFAST

Breakfast Surprise Muffins

Contributed by Helen Jacobs

Yield: 12 muffins   **Prep: 10 min**   **Cooking: 25 min**

- 2½ cups whole-wheat pastry flour (or 1 cup unbleached white flour for a slightly lighter muffin)
- 2 teaspoons baking powder
- 2 eggs, beaten
- ½ cup sunflower or safflower oil
- ½ cup + 1 tablespoon honey
- ½ cup milk
- 1 teaspoon vanilla extract
- 4 tablespoons favorite jam or preserves

Heat the oven to 350°. Grease a 12-muffin tin. In a mixing bowl, combine the flour and baking powder. In another bowl combine the eggs, oil, and honey. Mix well. Add the flour mixture to the egg mixture, and pour in the milk a little at a time. Add the vanilla extract and mix well. Be careful not to over-mix. Fill each muffin cup about half full of batter. Drop a scant teaspoon of jam in the center of the batter, and cover with the rest of the batter. Bake for 25 minutes.

Variations: Replace the vanilla extract with almond or lemon extract. Instead of the jam surprise, add ½ cup of dried cranberries and ¼ cup of chopped almonds or walnuts to the batter, fill the muffin cups and bake.

Chili Corn Muffins

Contributed by Carolyn Carleton

Yield: 12 muffins   **Prep: 30 min**   **Cooking: 40 min**

¼ cup onion, diced
½ cup fresh green chilies or 1 4-ounce can peeled green chilies, finely chopped
2 tablespoons pimento, diced
4 tablespoons (½ stick) butter, melted
3 ears fresh uncooked corn or 1½ cup frozen corn kernels
1 cup yellow cornmeal
1 cup white flour
1 tablespoon baking powder
1 teaspoon salt
¼ pound cheddar or Monterey Jack cheese, diced
1 cup milk
1 egg, lightly beaten

Preheat the oven to 350°. Sauté onion, green chilies, and pimento in 1 tablespoon of the butter, until onion is tender, about five minutes. In a mixing bowl, combine the cornmeal, flour, baking powder, and salt. Scrape the kernels from the corncobs and add to cornmeal mixture. Add the diced cheese. In another bowl, combine remaining butter with milk, egg, and cooked vegetables. Add the cornmeal mixture and stir until blended. Pour into greased muffin tins and bake for 40 minutes.

Citrus Heaven

Contributed by Cynthia Frank

Serves: 10   **Prep: 1 hr**

2 grapefruit
4 navel oranges
2 blood oranges
3 tangerines
2 tangelos
1 lemon
1 lime
2 cups sugar
¾ cup water
1 tablespoon honey

Zest all the fruit with a zesting tool or vegetable peeler. Cut the peels into strips ⅛ to ¼ inch wide. It's fine if the pieces are short. In a saucepan with 4 cups of cold water, place the strips and bring to a boil. Pour off the water and repeat the process. Set the blanched peel aside. In the same saucepan, combine the sugar and the water. Bring to a simmer and cook for 10 minutes. Add the peels and cook slowly while you prepare the fruit. Occasionally swirl or gently shake the pan. When the peel is translucent, use a slotted spoon to transfer peels to a small dish and set aside.

In a large mixing bowl, squeeze the juice from the lemon and lime and mix in the honey. With a sharp knife, remove the entire rind from the rest of the fruit and cut each in half lengthwise. Cut the halves crosswise into ¼-inch slices. Remove the seeds. Place sliced fruit in the bowl with the lemon and lime juice. Toss gently and taste. Add a little of the sugar syrup if you like it sweeter. Arrange the candied peel on top of the fruit and chill in refrigerator.

Variations: Add 2 to 3 Lavender Gems to the fruit mixture. Use whatever citrus is in season. Add a handful of kumquats, thinly sliced; 1 teaspoon fresh rosemary, chopped; or ½ teaspoon lavender, crushed.

Cottage Cheese Pancakes

Contributed by Carolyn Carleton

This may sound like an odd use of cottage cheese, but it is a delicious blintz-like breakfast food.

Serves: 4   **Prep: 10 min**

1 pound small curd cottage cheese
2 tablespoons sour cream
4 eggs
¼ cup sugar
1¼ cup flour
⅓ cup milk
½ cup blueberries or huckleberries *(optional)*

In a mixing bowl, combine all the ingredients and mix well. Melt a little butter on a griddle or frying pan on low heat and fry 3-inch diameter pancakes until browned on both sides. Serve with butter and maple syrup.

Daddy Mac's Flapjacks

Contributed by Daniel MacDonald

These are hearty, delicious, and healthy pancakes, full of protein, anti-oxidants, fiber, and wholesome goodness. You can fill your family's bellies and send them out into the world confident that they are well nourished and prepared for whatever lies ahead.

Serves: 4 to 6   **Prep: 30 min**

¾ cup whole wheat pastry flour
¼ cup almonds, ground until still a bit chunky
¼ cup quinoa flakes
1 tablespoon Sucanat or sugar
¾ teaspoon baking powder
¼ teaspoon baking soda
½ teaspoon cinnamon
¼ teaspoon nutmeg
pinch of cloves
dash of cardamom
¾ cup cottage cheese
¾ cup milk
4 egg whites
¾ teaspoon vanilla extract
12 ounces blueberries, fresh or thawed
1 cup walnuts, chopped

In a mixing bowl, combine the flour, almond meal, quinoa flakes, Sucanat, baking powder, baking soda, and spices, and mix well. Add the cottage cheese, milk, egg whites, and vanilla extract, and mix to form a thick batter. Fold in blueberries and walnuts. Melt a little butter on a griddle or frying pan on low heat and drop pancakes with ½-cup measure. Cook slowly. They will bubble on top when ready to flip, but not as much as thinner pancakes. Serve with maple syrup.

Variations: Substitute 1 tablespoon of lemon zest for the spices, ½ teaspoon of lemon extract and ½ teaspoon coconut extract for the vanilla extract, and slivered almonds for the walnuts. Top with Dickinson's Coconut Curd.

Overnight French Toast

Contributed by Cynthia Frank

Serves: 6 **Prep: 30 min** **Chilling: Overnight** **Baking: 40 - 45 min**

½ cup (1 stick) butter, melted
1 cup dark brown sugar
2 tablespoons molasses
6 large eggs
2½ cups milk
1½ teaspoon vanilla extract
1 cup pecans or walnuts, chopped
12 slices egg bread, sweet French bread, or challah
8 cups apples (Granny Smith, Gravenstein, Pippin, or Gala), cored, peeled, and
  thinly sliced
1 teaspoon cinnamon
½ teaspoon nutmeg

In a saucepan, combine the butter, brown sugar, and molasses. Bring just to the boiling point and pour into greased 9 x 13 pan. Sprinkle the butter mixture with chopped nuts. In a mixing bowl, beat eggs with milk and vanilla until foamy. Dip 6 slices of bread in egg mixture and place on the butter mixture. Cover with the apple slices. Dip the remaining bread slices in the egg mixture and place over the apples, aligning with the slices on the bottom layer. Pour the remaining egg mixture evenly over the top. Cover and place in refrigerator overnight.

Preheat oven to 350°. Sprinkle the slices with the cinnamon and nutmeg, and bake for 40 to 45 minutes. Serve immediately.

Variations: Replace the apples with raspberries, or use peaches and almonds in place of the apples and pecans or walnuts.

Spanish Tortilla

Contributed by Cynthia Frank

Serves: 4   **Prep: 30 min**

3 tablespoons olive oil
2 cups Yukon gold potatoes, red potatoes, or leftover cooked potatoes, diced
1 small yellow onion, sliced
⅓ cup Serrano ham, diced
1 roasted red pepper, roughly chopped
4 eggs
⅓ cup Manchego or Asiago cheese, grated
salt and pepper
Fresh parsley, chopped

Preheat oven to 375°. In a nonstick omelet pan, heat the olive oil over medium-high heat. Sauté the onions until they are soft and translucent, about 10 minutes. Add the potatoes and sauté until tender, about 3 minutes. Gently stir in the ham and peppers and cook for an additional 2 minutes.

In a large mixing bowl, add the eggs and whisk until well blended. Stir in the cheese until well mixed. Add the egg mixture to the pan, season with salt and pepper to taste, and gently stir with a heatproof spatula. Reduce the heat to low and cook until the eggs begin to thicken, about 2 minutes. Set the oven to broil and place the pan inside. Cook until the eggs are set and slightly puffed and golden on top, about 5 minutes.

Remove the pan from the oven and garnish with fresh parsley. Transfer to a serving platter, cut into wedges, and serve warm or at room temperature.

DRINKS

From Sue's Place: Whale Watch Bar at Little River

Contributed by Susan Bondoux

Sue, the bartender at Little River Inn Bar, puts up with two to eight of us every Wednesday. We stop there to eat and imbibe before rehearsal. Sue says, "There is a very tasty and refreshing drink called a Kamikaze. The basic recipe works for quite a few cocktails." Fill a cocktail shaker with crushed ice, add ingredients, and shake 40 times. This makes ice crystals float in the drink, making it super cold. Serve "up" in a martini glass and garnish with a lime wedge or anything that sounds fun.

Kamikaze

1¼ ounces vodka
1¼ ounces triple sec or Cointreau
1 splash Rose's Lime Juice

Cosmopolitan

1¼ ounces vodka
1¼ ounces triple sec or Cointreau
1 splash Rose's Lime Juice
Cranberry juice for color

Pomo Como

1¼ ounces vodka
1¼ ounces triple sec or Cointreau
1 splash Rose's Lime Juice

Rim glass with sugar and garnish with lemon wheel.

Purple Hooter

1¼ ounces vodka
1¼ ounces triple sec or Cointreau
1 splash Rose's Lime Juice
Chambord for color and raspberry flavor

Crystal Ruby

Serve this one over ice in a highball glass and garnish with lemon wheel and cherry.
1¼ ounces lemon vodka
1 splash Chambord
1 splash Tom Collins mix
1 splash 7-Up

Spiked Hot Chocolate

Spiked hot chocolate makes a terrific winter drink. Here are a few suggestions (don't forget the whipped cream):
1¼ ounces peppermint schnapps (garnish with candy cane), or
1¼ ounces Chambord, or
1¼ ounces cinnamon schnapps, or
1¼ ounces Grand Marnier (garnish with orange wheel)

Naomi's Ex-Mother-In-Law's Coffee Liqueur

Contributed by Naomi Feyer

This liqueur is lethal and goes down very easily, and a little goes a long way. It makes wonderful White Russians. For personal use, I usually cut the recipe in half and it lasts for many months. Bottled and labeled decoratively, it makes a great holiday gift. Buy several small dark glass bottles with caps or corks, and one batch can take care of most of your gift giving for the year.

Yield: 52 ounces **Prep: 15 min**

1½ cups water
1 2-ounce jar instant coffee
3½ cups white sugar
1½ tablespoons vanilla extract (not artificial)
26 ounces 90 or 100-proof vodka
(The higher proof means you can enjoy it immediately.)

In a large soup pot, boil the water and add the instant coffee. Stir until the coffee crystals are dissolved. Add the sugar and vanilla and mix thoroughly. Pour into a half-gallon bottle or jar and let cool. When the coffee mixture is cool, add vodka and shake until thoroughly mixed. Pour into dark-colored glass bottles, close the tops securely, and store away from direct sunlight.

APPETIZERS AND SNACKS

Five-Minute Chocolate Mug Cake

Contributed by Cheri Langlois

This is the most dangerous cake recipe in the world because now you are only five minutes away from chocolate cake at any time of the day or night.

Serves: 2   **Prep: 5 min**

4 tablespoons flour
4 tablespoons sugar
2 tablespoons cocoa
1 egg
3 tablespoons milk
3 tablespoons peanut or safflower oil
3 tablespoons chocolate chips *(optional)*
1 splash vanilla extract

In a large coffee mug (at least 16-ounce), combine the flour, sugar, and cocoa. Add the egg and mix thoroughly. Pour in the milk and oil and mix well. Add the chocolate chips and vanilla extract, and mix again. Put mug in the microwave and cook for 3 minutes at 1000 watts (high). The cake will rise over the top of the mug, but don't be alarmed. Let cool a little and tip out on to a plate, or eat directly from the mug.

Five-Pound Nachos

Contributed by Cheri Langlois

My sweetie and I would eat the whole thing watching a movie, but I have, under duress, shared with four others.

Serves: 2 to 5　　　　　　　　　　**Prep: 15 min**　　　　　　　　　**Baking: 15 min**

6 cups cheese, grated (2 cups cheddar, 2 cups jack, 2 cups your choice)
½ onion, chopped
½ 6-ounce can olives, pitted
1 teaspoon cumin
1 avocado, seeded, peeled, and mashed
1 cup chunky salsa
1 13-ounce bag tortilla chips
1 16-ounce container fat free sour cream

Preheat the oven to 250°. If the olives are whole, cut them in half. Cover the bottom of a 7 x 10 inch baking pan with tortilla chips and sprinkle with each kind of cheese until the chips are covered. Sprinkle the onion and olives on top, along with a bit of cumin. Cover with another layer of tortilla chips and repeat, and then do this for a third layer. Put pan in oven and bake for 15 minutes or until the cheese has melted. In a serving bowl, combine the avocado, salsa, and a teaspoon of cumin. Place the sour cream in another bowl or leave in container. Take the pan out of the oven, put on eating surface with a pad underneath, place the sour cream and guacamole close by, and dig in. Napkins recommended.

Holiday Nuts

Contributed by Cheri Langlois

This was my mother's favorite thing to serve as a snack at the holidays. I bring it to the Christmas Eve Poker Party every year.

Yield: 6 cups   **Prep: 45 min**   **Baking: 20 min**

½ cup butter (1 stick), melted
¼ cup Worcestershire sauce
1 teaspoon salt
6 cups of walnuts and pecans (halves or pieces)

Preheat the oven to 250°. In a small bowl, combine the butter, Worcestershire sauce, and salt and mix well. In a mixing bowl, add the nuts and pour in the butter mixture. Stir until nuts are coated (a plastic bowl scraper works best). Spread the nuts evenly on a cookie sheet and bake for 20 minutes. Check to see that the nuts are roasted (careful, they're hot). If not, bake for another 5 to 10 minutes. Let cool on cookie sheet, then peel off with a spatula, separate, and place in a serving bowl.

Variation: For the sweet version, replace Worcestershire sauce with ½ cup of honey or agave, and omit the salt. Follow the above directions.

Hot Artichoke Dip (Low-Fat Version)

Contributed by Kathleen MacDonald

This is a decadent appetizer and always welcome at potlucks and parties. It requires great discipline to limit yourself to just one serving.

Serves: 10   **Prep: 20 min**   **Baking: 20 - 25 min**

- 1 16-ounce package frozen artichoke hearts, thawed and drained (or 1 14-ounce can artichoke heart pieces in water, drained)
- 1 cup low fat mayonnaise
- 1 cup low fat sour cream
- 1 4-ounce can diced green chilies or jalapeños
- 1 shallot, diced
- 1 cup Parmesan cheese, shredded
- ¼ cup scallions (green onions), diced
- 1 whole-grain baguette, sliced thin
- Paprika *(optional)*

Preheat the oven to 350°. In the bowl of a food processor, place artichoke hearts and process to coarse chop. Add the mayonnaise, sour cream, chilies, and shallot, and process until smooth. Add the cheese and stir until mixed well. Pour into a shallow baking dish lightly sprayed with olive oil and sprinkle with scallions. Dust with the paprika and bake for 20 to 25 minutes or until bubbling. Serve warm with sliced baguette.

Variation: Fold in 4 ounces of fresh, cooked Dungeness crab pieces after baking.

Knock 'Em Dead Tuna Sandwich

Contributed by Jewels Marcus

Do you know how much hard work it takes to sing in this choir? These women are dedicated, glorious, inspired, and talented. (I'm still trying to find out whether I'm a high or low alto.)

Serves: 4   **Prep: 10 min**

4 6-ounce cans tuna, drained
¼ cup Annie's Organic Cowgirl Ranch Dressing
1 apple, cored, peeled, and chopped
2 celery stalks, chopped
4 bagels

In a mixing bowl, combine all the ingredients and mix well. You know how to make a sandwich.

Marvelous Mushrooms Appetizer

Contributed by Myra Beals

These are delicious with barbecued meats and roasts.

Serves: 4 to 6　　　　　**Prep: 15 min**　　　　　**Baking: 1 hr**

1 pound mushrooms, fresh
⅓ cup softened butter, unsalted
1 tablespoon fresh parsley, minced
1 tablespoon onion, minced
1 tablespoon Dijon mustard
1 teaspoon salt
pinch cayenne pepper
pinch ground nutmeg
1 tablespoon flour
1 cup heavy cream

Preheat the oven to 375°. Wash mushrooms and cut off stem ends. In a mixing bowl, cream the butter, parsley, onion, mustard, salt, cayenne pepper, nutmeg, and flour together. Place mushrooms in a 1-quart casserole dish and dot with the butter mixture. Pour the cream over the mushrooms and bake for about 1 hour uncovered. Stir once or twice during baking.

Mushroom Paté

Contributed by Karin Uphoff

Serves: 8   **Prep: 25 min**   **Cooking: 1 - 1½ hrs**

1 tablespoon olive oil

5 cups (1½ pounds) mushrooms, chopped (a combination of wild, shitake, and
    crimini is nice)

2 stalks celery, chopped

dash white wine or sherry

¼ teaspoon salt

1 cup breadcrumbs (regular or gluten-free)

½ cup chopped walnuts

⅓ cup tahini

2 tablespoons tamari

2 teaspoons herbes de Provence, or combination of fresh herbs

1 teaspoon tarragon

2 cloves garlic, crushed

⅔ cup scallions (green onions), chopped

½ teaspoon cayenne pepper

½ teaspoon black pepper

In a skillet, heat the oil and add the mushrooms, celery, wine, and salt. Lightly
sauté until mushrooms are soft and diminished in water content. In the bowl of
a food processor, combine the mushroom mixture with breadcrumbs, walnuts,
tahini, tamari, herbs, tarragon, garlic, scallions, cayenne pepper, and black pepper.
Blend until a smooth paste is formed.

Preheat the oven to 375°. Smooth mixture into a well-oiled loaf pan lined with
wax paper, smoothing out evenly. Bake for 1 to 1½ hours until firm but not dried
out (the edges will pull away from the pan a bit). Remove from oven and turn out
on a plate and chill.

Serve with a sprinkle of finely chopped parsley and your favorite cracker.

Roberta's "Pop in the Mouth" Appetizers

Contributed by Roberta Morrow

Little Boats

Serves: 6 to 8   **Prep: 20 min**

Fillings
- 1½ cups hummus
- 1½ cups herbed cream cheese
- ½ cup cream cheese, ½ cup plain yogurt, and ½ cup mayonnaise, mixed thoroughly
- ½ cup blue cheese, ½ cup Greek yogurt, 2 tablespoons Miracle Whip, dash Worcestershire sauce, mixed thoroughly
- ½ cup blue cheese, ½ cup softened cream cheese, and ½ cup yogurt, mixed thoroughly

Add a tablespoon minced garlic, onion, parsley, chives, or olives (black or green) to any of the above.

Garnishes
- 1 box cherry tomatoes, halved
- 1 box yellow pear tomatoes, halved
- 1 cup parsley, chopped
- Paprika

1 head organic romaine lettuce

Separate the lettuce into individual leaves. Set aside the smaller leaves and save the rest for a salad. Holding a smaller leaf, or "little boat" in one hand, spread 1 teaspoon of the chosen filling inside. Garnish with cherry or pear tomato half. Arrange boats on platter and sprinkle with parsley or paprika. Place ¼ to ½ cup of the filling in the center of the platter, create a border with the remaining tomato halves around the edge, and lay the boats around the tomatoes in a flower pattern.

Caprese

Serves: 4 to 6   **Prep: 10 min**

  1 pound Mozzarella cheese, sliced
  1 box cherry tomatoes, halved
  1 bunch fresh basil, sliced

Top 1 slice of Mozzarella cheese with tomato half and 1 slice of basil leaf. Arrange on plate and serve. Drizzle with olive oil for an extra authentic caprese.

Stuffed Dates

Serves: 8 to 10   **Prep: 15 min**

  1 8-ounce box dates, pitted
  ½ cup blue cheese, crumbled

Open the date and place ½ teaspoon blue cheese inside. Arrange on plate and serve.

Stuffed Date Appetizers with Balsamic Vinegar Sauce

Contributed by Carolyn Carleton

Before stuffing the dates, make the sauce in well-ventilated kitchen—the vinegar vapors are strong.

Serves: 12   **Prep: 45 min**

- 18 large Medjool dates, pitted
- 18 almonds, raw
- 8 ounces goat cheese
- 9 slices bacon, halved

Prepare a grill or preheat broiler in oven. Pack goat cheese around each almond and stuff inside each pitted date. Wrap bacon around each date and secure with a toothpick. Grill for 3 to 5 minutes per side until browned or broil in oven until browned on both sides. Drizzle balsamic sauce over the dates while hot and serve.

Balsamic Vinegar Sauce

- 2 cups balsamic vinegar
- 2 tablespoons butter

In a saucepan, simmer vinegar over low heat until thickened, about 20 minutes. Remove from heat and whisk in butter until smooth.

Tzimmis

Contributed by Karen Rakofsky

There are endless variations of tzimmis, a traditional Jewish dish often served on holidays. This version is a simple vegetable side dish that I've adapted from my mother's recipe. Tzimmis will last in the refrigerator for quite a few days, and works fine as a cold side dish for lunch.

Serves: 6 to 8   **Prep: 15 min**   **Cooking: 40 min**

1½ pounds carrots
1½ pounds yams, peeled
1 cup orange juice
9 dried apricots and/or prunes, chopped
½ teaspoon cinnamon

Preheat the oven to 350°. Cut carrots and yams into large chunks. In a heavy 4-quart saucepan, steam the vegetables until they are soft enough to easily mash. In a mixing bowl, combine the vegetables and mash, adding the orange juice a little at a time. Add the dried fruit and cinnamon and mix well.

Spread mixture into a lightly oiled 2-quart baking dish. Bake covered for 30 minutes. Remove the cover and bake for another 10 minutes. Serve while hot.

Zucchini Rolls

Contributed by Melanie Barrett, Owner and Chef,
Pacific Tapas Company, Little River

Yield: 5 rolls   **Prep: 15 min**

5 slices zucchini, cut thin lengthwise

5 julienne slices roasted red bell peppers

5 sprigs of chives

5 ounces herbed goat cheese (plain soft goat cheese seasoned with 1 tablespoon
   thyme, chopped, and 1 tablespoon rosemary, chopped.)

To cut the zucchini into slices, trim off the ends and slice lengthwise as thin as
you can (a mandoline slicer is helpful in doing this). Lay out the zucchini slices.
Place 1 ounce goat cheese, a slice of red bell pepper, and a sprig of chive folded in
half on 1 zucchini slice. Begin 1 inch from the end of the slice and roll. Repeat for
the remaining slices.

SOUPS

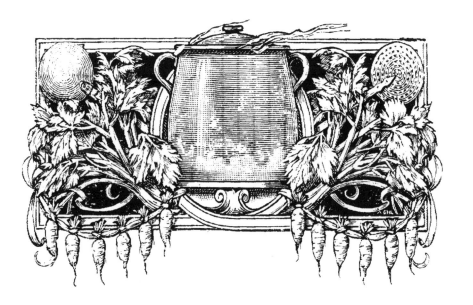

Curried Sweet Potato and Cauliflower Soup

Contributed by Jeannette Rasker

This low fat, vegan, flavorful, creamy soup is welcome during any season, but it goes down really well on a rainy winter day.

Serves: 6 to 8   **Prep: 1 hr 15 min**

2 tablespoons grape seed oil or olive oil
2 onions, finely chopped
2 teaspoons fresh ginger, grated
1½ teaspoons curry powder
1 teaspoon cumin
Pinch cayenne pepper or red pepper flakes *(optional)*
1 cauliflower, cut into small pieces
2 medium sweet potatoes cut into small pieces
  (I prefer the Japanese sweet potatoes.)
5 cups vegetable broth
½ teaspoon apple cider vinegar, or more to taste
Salt and black pepper to taste

In a heavy 4-quart saucepan, heat the oil on low to medium heat and add the onions and ginger. Cook until the onions are soft and translucent, about 10 minutes. Turn the heat down to low, and add the curry powder, cumin, and cayenne pepper. Stir well and keep stirring for about 3 minutes. Add the sweet potatoes and the cauliflower and stir for 2 minutes longer. Add the vegetable broth and the apple cider vinegar and turn up the heat until the soup comes to a boil. Simmer on low for 30 minutes, or until the vegetables are thoroughly cooked.

Transfer the vegetable mixture to a blender and purée. A food processor works great as well. Check for flavor, and add salt, pepper, and more curry powder according to your taste. If the soup is too thick, add a bit more broth. Reheat soup on low heat and garnish each serving with a sprinkling of chopped fresh cilantro and 1 tablespoon of sour cream or plain yogurt.

Hearty Vegetable Soup

Contributed by Karen Rakofsky

You can use a variety of vegetables in this soup, including broccoli, cauliflower, green beans, and peas. Leave out the wine and parsnips, substitute kale for chard, and use fewer potatoes and yams.

Serves: 12 **Prep: 30 min** **Cooking: 1½ hrs**

1½ pounds yam, sliced
½ pound Yukon Gold or red
potatoes, sliced
1½ quarts water
1 quart vegetable stock
2 tablespoons olive oil
1½ large onions, chopped
½ pound mushrooms, sliced
6 cloves garlic, minced
1 teaspoon basil
1 teaspoon thyme
½ teaspoon dill
1 teaspoon marjoram
½ teaspoon salt
1 large parsnip, thinly sliced
2 large carrots, thinly sliced
2 tomatoes, chopped
2 stalks celery, chopped
1 bunch Swiss chard, stems
removed, coarsely chopped
1 cup Chardonnay, Chenin
Blanc, or white table wine
¾ cup corn *(optional)*
Salt and black pepper to taste

In a heavy 4-quart saucepan, combine the yam and potatoes with stock and water. Bring to a boil, then lower to a simmer. When all are soft, turn off heat.

Meanwhile, in a skillet, sauté the onions, mushrooms, and garlic in olive oil. Stir occasionally. Add a small amount of water if the vegetables stick to the skillet. Cook until the onions are soft and translucent, about 10 minutes. Add basil, thyme, dill, marjoram, and salt, stirring well. Add the carrots and parsnips, then add the celery, chard, and tomatoes and stir occasionally. Cook covered for 15 minutes, or until all the vegetables are done. Turn the heat back on under the saucepan and add the contents of the skillet. Bring to a boil, then lower to a simmer. Cook for 30 minutes. Add the wine and corn and cook for 10 minutes. Add the salt and pepper. Serve hot or let cool and reheat over the next few days for an even heartier flavor.

Minted Pea and Spinach Soup

Contributed by June Lemos

This pretty green soup is perfect for a cold winter's day, or St. Patrick's. Serve it with a green salad and a crusty loaf of French bread. Do not be alarmed if you hear the "Hallelujah Chorus" after the first taste. It's in the mint.

Serves: 8   **Prep: 1 hr**

½ cup (1 stick) butter
4 cups onion, diced
2 10-ounce packages frozen spinach, thawed and drained
6 cups vegetable stock or broth
2 10-ounce packages frozen peas, thawed
4 cups (1 to 2 bunches) fresh mint leaves
1½ cups cream
Salt and black pepper to taste

In a heavy stockpot, melt butter. Add the onions and cook over low heat, partly covered, for 25 minutes. Add the spinach, vegetable stock, and peas. Bring to a boil and then lower the heat to simmer for 5 minutes. Add the mint leaves and simmer for another 5 minutes. Pour soup through a strainer and reserve the liquid. In a blender or food processor, blend the soup until smooth, adding half of the reserved liquid a little at a time. Return pureed soup to the pot and whisk in the cream and enough of the remaining liquid until you reach the desired consistency. Add the salt and black pepper to taste. Bring back up to temperature and serve hot.

Peasant Soup

Contributed by Cheri Langlois

Serves: 8   **Prep: 2 hrs**

1 28-ounce can diced tomatoes (Muir Farms Fire-Roasted)
3 medium Yukon Gold or russet potatoes, diced
4 carrots, diced
½ cup dried aduki beans, black beans, or black-eyed peas
3½ cups water
2 tablespoons olive oil
½ onion, diced
1 red bell pepper, diced
3 stalks celery, diced
3 cloves garlic, minced
Curry powder

In large soup pot on low heat, combine the tomatoes, beans, and water. Add the carrots and potatoes, and let simmer. In a skillet on low heat, add the olive oil, onion, bell pepper, celery, and garlic. Sauté until the onion is translucent and cara-melized. Sprinkle the mixture with curry powder according to your taste.

Add the vegetable mixture to the soup pot. Cover and let cook on medium/low heat for 1 hour. Stir once or twice and check to see if it needs more water. Cook until carrots and potatoes are soft and beans are cooked. It doesn't have to boil.

If you want to make it a bit Italian, replace the curry with oregano. When the soup is close to being done, add 1 9-ounce package of prepared tortellini or ravi-oli. Heat until pasta is cooked. Serve either soup with shredded Parmesan cheese sprinkled on top.

Roasted Carrot Soup

Contributed by Sari Scanlon

Serves: 8   **Prep: 1 hr**

8 or 9 large carrots, thickly sliced
1 medium onion, coarsely chopped
1 large stalk celery, thickly sliced
1 tablespoon olive oil
½ teaspoon salt
8 cups chicken or vegetable stock
⅓ cup Madeira
White pepper

Preheat the oven to 400°. In a mixing bowl, toss carrots, onion, and celery in olive oil and salt. Spread vegetables on a baking sheet and roast in the oven for 20 minutes, or until the carrots are brown and blister. In a heavy 4-quart saucepan, bring the stock to a boil and add the roasted vegetables. Simmer for 10 minutes or until the carrots fluff up and are soft. Add the Madeira and simmer for 3 more minutes. Let cool for 10 minutes and then pour the mixture into a blender and puree until very smooth. Season to taste with white pepper.

Uncle Paul's Lentil Soup

Contributed by Susan Fraser

One of my favorite memories of visiting my great aunt was that her German husband, Paul, always had his lentil soup on the stove when I arrived. It keeps well in the fridge for several days and also freezes well. I always double the recipe.

Serves: 4   **Prep: 45 min**   **Cooking: 2 hrs**

1½ cups lentils
6 cups water
5 strips bacon, chopped
2 cups celery, chopped
1 cup carrots, chopped
3 cloves garlic, chopped
1 cup Yukon Gold potatoes, diced
2 cloves
2 bay leaves
4 cups beef stock
1 teaspoon salt
2 teaspoons Accent
Black pepper
2 tablespoons red wine vinegar
2 cups garlic sausage, sliced
1 cup leeks, sliced *(optional)*

In a mixing bowl, combine the lentils and water and let soak overnight. Rinse and drain the lentils before using. In a skillet, combine the bacon along with the onion, celery, carrots, and garlic, and sauté for 10 minutes or until the onions are translucent. In a soup pot, combine the vegetables with the lentils and other ingredients except for the vinegar, sausage, and leeks. Cover and simmer for 1½ hours, stirring occasionally. Add the vinegar, sausage, and leek to the soup and cook long enough to heat sausage. Serve hot.

Winter Squash Chestnut Soup

Contributed by Rachel Lahn

Serves: 6   Prep: 1 hr   Cooking: 2¼ hrs

1 medium butternut or other winter squash
3 tablespoons olive oil
1 sweet potato
20 chestnuts
2 medium onions, chopped
4 cloves garlic
2 carrots, sliced
½ teaspoon ground cardamom
½ teaspoon cumin
½ teaspoon cinnamon
½ teaspoon nutmeg
hot chile pepper
1-inch fresh ginger, peeled and grated or ¾ teaspoon ground ginger
1 teaspoon black mustard seeds
Salt to taste
3½ cups water
Juice of 1 large or 2 medium lemons

Preheat the oven to 375°. Cut the squash in half lengthwise and remove any seeds. Rub 1 tablespoon of the olive oil on the inside. Place the squash facedown on the baking sheet along with the sweet potato and bake for 45 minutes or until soft. Mash the squash and set aside. Peel the sweet potato and cut into chunks, and set aside. Slit the skins of the chestnuts. In a skillet on medium heat, roast the chestnuts until they crack open, shaking occasionally. In a soup pot, heat the remaining oil and sauté the onions, garlic, carrots, and spices until onions are translucent. Add the water, squash, sweet potato, and chestnuts. Bring to a slow boil and then cover and simmer for 1½ hours. In a blender, pour the soup mixture and blend to your desired consistency. Add the lemon juice before serving.

Zattu's Butternut Squash Soup

Contributed by Zattu Kadan

Serves: 6   **Prep: 1½ hrs**

1 large butternut squash
3 tablespoons olive oil
1 large onion, chopped
3 cloves garlic, minced
1-inch piece fresh ginger, peeled and finely chopped
2 apples, chopped
1 teaspoon curry powder
½ teaspoon ground cinnamon
3 cups water
1 14-ounce can light coconut milk
Salt and black pepper to taste

Preheat the oven to 400°. Cut the squash in half lengthwise and remove the seeds. Rub 1 tablespoon of the olive oil on cut surfaces and place in baking dish with the cut surfaces up. Bake for 1 hour, or until the squash is very soft. Remove meat from skin and set aside. In a large heavy saucepan, heat the remaining olive oil and sauté the onion, garlic, and ginger until the onion is translucent, about 10 minutes. Add the apples, curry, and cinnamon, and continue to sauté until the apples are soft. Add the squash and mix well.

In a food processor or blender, puree the squash mixture in batches, adding water as needed. Mixture should be quite thick. Return to saucepan and heat until simmering. Let simmer for 5 to 10 minutes, stirring occasionally. Add the coconut milk, stir, bring back to simmer to heat through and blend flavors. Do not let boil. Add the salt and pepper to taste and garnish individual servings with a dollop of yogurt or sour cream.

If time is short, peel and cut the squash into chunks and boil until soft, and drain. However, for a superb tasting soup, baking is best. Squash may also be baked the night before.

SIDE DISHES

Baked BBQ Black Beans

Recipe from Robert Goleman

This rich and hearty side dish is great with barbequed chicken or ribs, and is quick and easy to prepare. Make ahead and refrigerate overnight before baking for an even richer flavor.

Serves: 8 to 10   **Prep: 20 min**   **Cooking: 1 hr**

12 ounces peppered bacon
1 medium yellow onion, diced
1 small red bell pepper, diced
2 medium celery stalks, diced
2 medium carrots (unpeeled), diced
3 cloves garlic, minced
3 15-ounce cans black beans, slightly drained (reserve some of the liquid)
½ cup ketchup
½ cup molasses
½ cup brown sugar
2 tablespoons brown or prepared mustard (not Dijon)
2 tablespoons fresh parsley, finely chopped

Set aside 5 strips of the bacon and cut the remaining strips into half-inch pieces. In a large skillet, fry the bacon pieces until they are crispy. Remove the bacon and place in a large mixing bowl, and leave the drippings in the skillet. Over medium-high heat, sauté the onion in the bacon drippings until the onion is translucent, about 10 minutes. Add the bell pepper, celery, carrots, and garlic, and sauté for another 5 minutes. Remove from the heat and pour the mixture into the bowl with the bacon. Add the rest of the ingredients (except reserved, uncooked bacon) to the bowl, and stir until well mixed. Pour the beans into a large, covered casserole. Arrange the reserved bacon strips on top of the beans and put on the lid. At this stage, the beans may be refrigerated until baking time, or even a few days.

Preheat the oven to 350° and bake the beans covered for 30 minutes. Remove the cover and bake for another 30 minutes, or until the bacon on top is done and the beans are bubbling. Serve immediately with warm cornbread.

Barley Casserole

Contributed by Babs Levine

Serves: 6 to 8   **Prep: 10 min**   **Baking: 1½ hrs**

½ cup (1 stick) butter
1 cup pearl barley
1 cup mushrooms, sliced
2 cups chicken broth
½ 2-ounce package onion soup mix
1 cup almonds, sliced
2 tablespoons white wine or sherry

Preheat the oven to 350°. In a skillet, melt the butter and brown the barley and mushrooms. Add the remaining ingredients, mix well, and place in a greased casserole dish. Cover and bake for 1½ hours. Stir once or twice during cooking time.

Citrus Coleslaw

Contributed by Nancy Fereira

Serves: 6   **Prep: 20 min**

2½ cups red cabbage, thinly sliced
½ cup carrot, grated
1 small Granny Smith apple, peeled and grated
Salt

Dressing

⅓ cup fresh orange juice
½ Meyer lemon, juice only, about 2 tablespoons
½ cup mayonnaise
1 tablespoon lemon pepper

In a mixing bowl, combine the cabbage, carrot, and apple. Mix well and add salt to taste. In a separate bowl, combine the dressing ingredients, mix well, and stir into cabbage mixture. Serve chilled.

Crab and Artichoke Salad

Contributed by Babs Levine

I have always thought of this very easy and delicious salad as a lady's luncheon salad.

Serves: 4   **Prep: 15 min**

- 1 13-ounce can crabmeat
- 1 6-ounce jar artichoke hearts in oil
- 1 tablespoon lemon juice
- 2 tablespoons chives or scallions (green onions), minced
- 1 cup sour cream
- 1 head Bibb lettuce, separated into leaves
- 1 tomato, sliced
- 1 avocado, peeled, seeded, and sliced
- 1 medium carrot, cut into strips

In a mixing bowl, combine the crabmeat, artichoke hearts, lemon juice, chives, and sour cream. Mix well. To serve, place mound of the crabmeat mixture on a bed of lettuce and garnish with avocado, tomato wedges, and carrot.

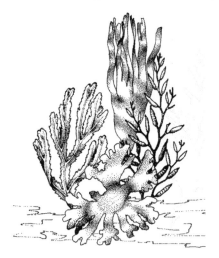

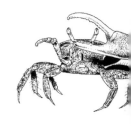

Microwave Cauliflower

Contributed by Babs Levine

Serves: 6   **Prep: 20 min**

1 whole cauliflower
½ cup mayonnaise
1 tablespoon dehydrated onion, minced
1 tablespoon prepared mustard
½ cup cheddar cheese, grated

Place cauliflower on glass pie plate and microwave on high for 5 to 7 minutes, or until soft (it should give when you squeeze it). In a mixing bowl, combine the mayonnaise, onion, and mustard and slather the mixture on cauliflower. Sprinkle with cheese and microwave on high for an additional minute until the cheese has melted. Cut in wedges to serve.

Mother's Rice Dressing

Contributed by Cheri Langlois

This is the dressing I remember from my childhood Thanksgivings, and into adulthood.

Serves: 8 to 10   **Prep: 30 min**   **Cooking: 1 hr**

2 cups rice (basmati, long grain brown, and wild rice)
2 tablespoons olive oil
6 stalks celery, chopped
½ onion, chopped
2 cloves garlic, minced
¼ cup butter (½ stick), softened
2 cups almonds, toasted and sliced

Heat oven to 350°. In a heavy 4-quart saucepan, cook rice in 4 cups of water until it is about half done (roughly 10 minutes from when it begins to boil). In a skillet, heat the olive oil and sauté the celery, onion, and garlic until the celery is barely tender. Pour the remaining water from the rice into a 2-quart Pyrex baking dish. Add the celery mixture and butter, and stir until well mixed. Cover baking dish with lid and bake for 20 minutes. Lower oven to 200° and remove baking dish. Add 1 cup of the almonds, mix well, and return to oven for 10 minutes. Before serving, sprinkle the rice dressing with the remaining 1 cup of almonds.

Rachel's Cabbage Rolls

Contributed by Babs Levine

Rachel was the mother-in-law I never met, but I came by her recipes and a few of her pots. This is one of my husband's favorites.

Serves: 8   **Prep: 30 min**   **Cooking: 3½ hrs**

1 medium green cabbage
1 pound ground beef
1 onion, minced
1 cup rice, cooked
1 28-ounce can solid pack tomatoes, chopped
½ cup brown sugar
½ cup golden raisins
Salt and pepper to taste

Preheat the oven to 300°. In a large soup pot, cover the cabbage with hot water and bring to a boil. In a skillet, brown the beef and onion, and then add the cooked rice. Add salt and pepper to taste. Remove the cabbage from the water and let cool until you can handle it. Separate the leaves and fill each with a spoonful of meat mixture, and roll into balls. Place the balls into a 9 x 12 baking dish. Chop the remaining cabbage and sprinkle over the balls. In a mixing bowl, combine the tomatoes, brown sugar, and raisins. Mix well and spread over the balls. Cover with foil and bake for 3½ hours.

Rosemary Potatoes

Contributed by Donna Feiner

Serves: 6   **Prep: 10 min**   **Cooking: 1½ hrs**

6 medium Yukon Gold potatoes, halved and cut into 3 wedges per half
¼ cup olive oil
1 tablespoon rosemary
1½ teaspoons garlic powder
1½ teaspoons salt

Preheat the oven to 400°. In a large mixing bowl, combine the ingredients and mix well. Spread the potatoes on as many baking trays that will fit the top shelf of your oven. Bake for 1½ hours, turning the potatoes every half hour. I usually triple this basic recipe for potlucks.

Sally's Famous Potato Chard Casserole

Contributed by Sally Fletcher

Serves: 6 to 8   **Prep: 30 min**   **Cooking: 40 min**

6 russet potatoes, peeled and cut into half-inch thick slices
1 bunch Swiss chard, stems removed, coarsely chopped
1 tablespoon olive oil
10 button or crimini mushrooms, sliced
3 stalks celery, chopped
4 green onions, chopped
¾ cup salsa
1 cup sour cream
1 cup mild cheddar cheese, grated

Preheat the oven to 350°. In a large saucepan, steam potatoes for 20 minutes. Remove potatoes and steam chard for 5 minutes. In a skillet, heat the olive oil and combine the mushrooms with onions and celery. Sauté until the mushrooms are cooked. In medium casserole dish, layer the salsa, potatoes, chard, mushroom mixture, and sour cream. Put on another layer of potato and salsa and top with the cheese. Bake for 40 minutes.

Sweet Potato Salad

Contributed by Nancy Fereira

Serves: 8 to 10   **Prep: 40 min**   **Cooking: 20 min**   **Chilling: 2 hrs**

2 pounds garnet yams, peeled and diced
2 tablespoons butter, melted
1 teaspoon salt
¼ teaspoon nutmeg or cinnamon
1 cup mayonnaise
2 tablespoons honey
½ teaspoon ground ginger
2 tablespoons orange juice
¼ teaspoon orange zest
¾ cup celery, chopped
¾ cup pecans, toasted
¼ cup green onions, sliced
¾ cup cranberries or raisins

Preheat the oven to 350°. In a mixing bowl, combine the yams, butter, salt, and nutmeg. Spread on a baking sheet and bake for 20 minutes or until fork tender. In another mixing bowl, combine the mayonnaise, honey, ground ginger, orange juice, and orange zest. Mix well and add the celery, pecans, onions, and cranberries. Mix well and add the potatoes while they are still warm. Mix again and place in the refrigerator. Serve chilled.

Zattu's Favorite Winter Salad

Contributed by Zattu Kadan

I make this sweet salad in the wintertime when we don't have access to organic homegrown tomatoes. It's become a real family favorite.

Serves: 6   **Prep: 15 min**

1 small head green leaf lettuce or romaine, washed and torn into small pieces
2 navel or Valencia oranges, peeled, seeded, and chopped
1 ripe avocado, peeled, seeded, and cut into chunks

Line a salad bowl with lettuce and place oranges and avocado on top.

Dressing

½ cup plain yogurt
⅓ cup mayonnaise
3 tablespoons ketchup
2 teaspoons prepared mustard (brown
    or Dijon)
2-3 tablespoons water

In a covered jar, combine the dressing ingredients and shake until well blended.
Pour over salad and serve.

Zucchini Heaven aka Smashed Squash

Contributed by Sari Scanlon

Sorry about the name, but it is official. When zucchini is prepared this way, even the pickiest eater in our family will eat this over-abundant and suspect vegetable.

Serves: 4   **Prep: 10 min**   **Cooking: 25 min**

3 tablespoons olive oil
1 sweet yellow onion, finely chopped
3 cloves garlic, minced
4 medium zucchini, diced
¼ teaspoon turmeric
1 teaspoon salt
1 teaspoon cumin
Pinch cayenne pepper
1 tablespoon tomato paste

In a skillet, heat the olive oil and sauté onions and garlic for 10 minutes, or until translucent. Add the zucchini and turmeric and cook for another 10 minutes, or until zucchini is soft. Add the salt, cumin, cayenne pepper and tomato paste and stir well. Using a potato masher, mash the squash and serve hot.

SAUCES AND CONDIMENTS

Chervil Pesto

Contributed by Cynthia Frank

Yield: 2¼ cups   **Prep: 30 min**

2 cups fresh chervil, packed
½ cup Romano or Pecorino cheese
¼ cup toasted pine nuts
⅓ cup olive oil
2 cloves garlic, crushed
Zest of 1 lemon

In a large mixing bowl, add 4 cups of water and half a tray of ice cubes. In a large saucepan, bring 6 cups of water to a boil. Place the chervil in a strainer that fits into the saucepan and plunge the strainer into the boiling water. Push down the leaves so they blanch evenly. Count to 15, remove strainer from saucepan and plunge into the ice water. This stops the cooking and preserves the color. Drain chervil immediately and place into food processor. Add cheese, pine nuts, olive oil, garlic, and lemon zest. Pulse till smooth. Serve over pasta, baste on fish or chicken, or paint onto flatbreads or baguettes before broiling. Freezes well, too.

Cranberry Sauce with Amaretto

Contributed by Jeannette Rasker

This sauce is great with turkey or chicken, of course, but is also good on pancakes, toast, and even in plain yogurt.

Serves: 8 to 10 people   **Prep: 15 min**

4 cups cranberries, fresh or fresh-frozen
⅔ cup sugar
⅔ cup water
2 lemons, juice only
⅓ cup marmalade
⅓ cup amaretto
⅓ cup white almonds, pieces

In a stainless steel (non-reactive) saucepan, combine the cranberries, sugar, and water. Bring to a boil and cook softly while stirring until most of the cranberries have popped and the sauce starts to thicken, about 10 minutes. Remove the saucepan from the heat and add the lemon juice and the marmalade. Mix well. Transfer the sauce to a glass container and place in the refrigerator to cool thoroughly. When cool, add the amaretto and the almond pieces, and serve.

Jill's Pesto

Contributed by Jill Jahelka

Jill choreographed a can-can piece for the choir's 2010 season, and her pesto dishes are as famous as her high kicks. This recipe is a Lemos family favorite.

Serves: 6 to 8   **Prep: 20 min**

6 to 8 cloves garlic, peeled
¾ cup pine nuts
3 bunches fresh basil, washed, rinsed, and stems removed
¾ cup olive oil
¾ cup Parmesan or Romano cheese, shredded

In a food processor, combine the garlic and pine nuts in food processor and pulse until they are coarsely chopped. Add the basil and pulse. Drizzle in the olive oil and continue pulsing. Add the cheese and pulse until the ingredients are well mixed yet still have texture. Take off the top of the processor and taste. If the pesto is not quite there, add more garlic or pine nuts or add olive oil until you would be proud to serve it to your son's Italian girlfriend. Serve over warm pasta.

Meyer Lemon Gremolata

Contributed by Cynthia Frank

Yield: ½ cup   **Prep: 10 min**

1 medium or 2 small Meyer lemons (organic, since you'll be using the peel)
⅓ cup flat leaf parsley, finely chopped
3 cloves garlic, finely minced

Zest the lemon and finely chop the peel. If you don't have a good zester, a sharp vegetable peeler will work. In small mixing bowl, combine the zest, parsley, and garlic, and mix well. Sprinkle on soup, roast meat, chicken, fish, or grilled bread. Gremolata can also be pressed into ice cube tray cubes (1 tablespoon per cube) and frozen for later use.

Spicy Cranberry Chutney

Contributed by Nancy Roca

Try this chutney with pork and poultry, and quiche and crepes.

Yield: 2 cups   **Prep: 45 min**

4 cups cranberries, fresh or fresh-frozen
1 cup seedless raisins
1 cup water
1⅔ cup sugar
1 tablespoon cinnamon
1½ teaspoons ground ginger
¼ teaspoon ground cloves
1 medium onion, chopped
1 medium apple, chopped
½ cup celery, sliced

In a stainless steel (non-reactive) saucepan, combine the cranberries, raisins, water, sugar, cinnamon, ginger, and cloves. Cook over medium high heat until most of the cranberries have popped and mixture thickens, about 15 minutes. Add the onion, apple, and celery and mix well. Cook 15 minutes, stirring occasionally. Let cool and refrigerate in a closed container.

Sweet and Sour Onions

Contributed by Cynthia Frank

Serves: 4 to 6 as a side dish, or 8 as garnish for roast beef or pork   **Prep: 40 min**

3-4 small to medium yellow onions (1 pound), peeled
½ bay leaf
4 tablespoons butter
1 tablespoon olive oil
1 tablespoon brown sugar
1½ tablespoons red wine vinegar
1½ tablespoons balsamic vinegar
Pinch of salt

Cut the ends from the onions and quarter, and then cut crosswise. In a saucepan, bring 4 cups of water to boil. Add bay leaf. Add onion and boil gently in water to cover for 5 minutes. Drain and set aside.

In a skillet, melt the butter. Add the olive oil and onions, and cook slowly. After about 15 minutes the onions should start to brown. Keep cooking. When browned evenly, sprinkle with brown sugar. Stir in the red wine and balsamic vinegar, and mix well. Cover the skillet, reduce to low heat, and cook for about 5 minutes.

Uncover and stir gently. Add salt, stir again, and taste. The sauce should be dark and sticky. Adjust seasonings to your preference by adding more balsamic vinegar and brown sugar. (Much depends on the quality of the vinegars and the sweetness of the onions.) Can be served hot or cold.

Variations: Replace yellow onions with whole small boiling onions. Replace red wine vinegar with more balsamic vinegar. Add cracked black pepper to taste along with the salt.

MAIN DISHES

Birthday Gumbo

Contributed by Ledford House – for Maya and LuLu

Gumbo is a stew that originated in south Louisiana. Our gumbo consists primarily of chicken stock, a thickener, and the vegetable "holy trinity" of celery, bell peppers, and onion. Serve it over your best rice.

Serves: 8 to 10	Prep: 45 min	Cooking: 30 min

1 cup bacon or duck fat
1 cup flour
1½ pounds okra, cut into quarter-inch rounds
1 15-ounce can tomatoes, chopped
¾ cup onions, chopped
¾ cup celery, chopped
¾ cup green bell pepper, chopped
2 cloves garlic, crushed and chopped
4 tablespoons flat leaf parsley, chopped and divided
1 teaspoon dried thyme
1 teaspoon salt
½ teaspoon cayenne pepper
3 large bay leaves
1 quart water
1 quart chicken stock
2 pounds uncooked medium shrimp, peeled and de-veined
1 pound ham, diced
2 tablespoons scallions (green onions), sliced

In a heavy skillet, heat the fat on high heat until it begins to smoke. Gradually add the flour and whisk in with a long handled metal whisk. Continue cooking until the roux is a dark red-brown color, about 2 to 4 minutes. Add the okra and sauté, stirring constantly, for 15 minutes or until most of the slime is gone. Add the tomatoes, onion, celery, bell pepper, and garlic. Add half of the parsley, thyme, salt, cayenne pepper, bay leaves, water, and chicken stock. Stir and bring to a boil. Reduce the heat to medium and simmer for 15 minutes. Add the shrimp and ham, and cook for 20 minutes, stirring occasionally, or until the shrimp turn pink. Remove bay leaves. Serve over rice and garnish with scallions and the remaining parsley.

Buffalo Moussaka

Contributed by Sari Scanlon

Serves: 6 **Prep: 45 min** **Cooking: 30 min**

2 medium eggplant, sliced into half-inch rounds
¼ teaspoon cumin
¼ teaspoon salt
¼ teaspoon oregano
1 tablespoon olive oil
1 medium onion, sliced
1 red bell pepper, sliced
1 pound ground buffalo
1 clove elephant garlic, chopped coarsely
⅓ cup dry red wine
½ teaspoon cinnamon
1 bunch fresh basil, chopped
4 cups tomato sauce
1 cup Parmesan cheese, shredded

Preheat the oven to 400°. Coat baking sheet with olive oil and lay out eggplant rounds. Sprinkle with cumin, salt, and oregano. Bake for 30 minutes or until brown, remove and set aside. In a skillet, heat the olive oil and sauté onions until brown. Add the bell peppers and cook for 2 minutes. Add the buffalo and cook until not pink. Add the garlic, wine, cinnamon, and fresh basil. Cook for 2 more minutes and remove from the heat.

In a 9 x 13 baking dish, pour 1 cup of tomato sauce and spread to cover the bottom of the dish. Place the eggplant slices side by side on top of the tomato sauce. Spoon the buffalo mixture on top of the eggplant, cover with the tomato sauce again, and continue the layers until finished. Top with the cheese and bake for 30 minutes or until the cheese and sauce are bubbling.

Butternut Ravioli with Homemade Ricotta Cheese

Contributed by Tracey Coddington

This is a lot of fun to make with the dinner guests.

Serves: 8 to 10   **Prep: 2 hrs**

1 gallon whole milk
1 quart buttermilk
1 teaspoon salt
1 medium butternut squash
2 tablespoons olive oil
4 tablespoons fresh basil, finely cut
3 cloves garlic, crushed
2 tablespoons parsley
1 cup pecans, roasted and chopped
Salt and black pepper
1 package (80) wonton wrappers
2 egg whites
1 teaspoon butter
½ onion, finely chopped
1 28-ounce can crushed tomatoes
½ cup red wine
⅓ cup cream
¾ cup Parmesan cheese

For the ricotta: In a large saucepan, combine the milk, buttermilk, and salt, and heat to a boil. Stir constantly and as soon as the milk begins to curdle, scoop out the solids and place in a fine strainer or cheesecloth. Continue until the liquid turns slightly green and the curdling stops. Let the ricotta drain and set aside.

For the ravioli: Preheat the oven to 375°. Cut the squash in half lengthwise and remove any seeds. Rub 1 tablespoon of the olive oil on the inside. Place the squash facedown on baking sheet and bake for 45 minutes or until soft. In a mixing bowl, mash the squash and add the ricotta, half of the basil, garlic, pecans, and ½ cup of the Parmesan cheese. Mix well and season with salt and black pepper to your taste.

Arrange 10 wonton wrappers on a lightly floured surface. Brush egg white along the border of each wrapper and place a teaspoon of filling in each. Close them diagonally and seal edges with a fork just like the border of a pie. Cover the filled ravioli with a cotton towel and repeat with the next set of 10 until all the wrappers are filled. In a large soup pot, bring salted water to a gentle boil and cook until they rise to the top of the water. Extra ravioli can be frozen for later use by placing them on wax paper and sealed in a heavy-duty freezer bag, with wax paper in between each layer.

For the sauce: In a saucepan, heat the remaining olive oil and butter, and sauté the onion for 10 minutes or until translucent. Add the tomatoes, wine, and ½ teaspoon of salt, and cook for 30 minutes. Add the remaining basil, cream, and remaining Parmesan cheese just before serving. Spoon over ravioli and serve.

Chicken and Mushrooms

Contributed by Sydelle Lapidus

I learned this from my roommate, Philippa Claude, in 1962. She was half-Belgian and spent much of her time in Europe. I thought it was the most sophisticated dish I had encountered in all my 20 years.

Serves: 6   **Prep: 90 min**

1½ tablespoons olive oil
1 tablespoon butter
1 large chicken, cut in 8 pieces
½ to ¾ pounds mushrooms, cleaned and sliced
5 scallions (green onions), sliced crosswise
¼ cup white wine
Salt and black pepper

In a large skillet, heat the olive oil and butter, and brown the chicken pieces on each side. If all the pieces don't fit in the pan at one time, do this in batches. Place the mushrooms and scallions on top of the chicken, and add the wine and cover. Simmer until chicken is cooked, about 20 minutes. Add salt and pepper to taste before serving. Be careful not to overcook, as there is nothing worse than dry chicken.

Chicken or Pork with Dried-Fruit Cider Sauce

Contributed by Nancy Fereira

Thanks to Marilou, for your wonderful dried fruit that inspired this recipe.

Serves: 6   **Prep: 40 min**

2 pork tenderloins, silver skin removed and cut in 1¼ inch slices or
4 to 6 boneless, skinless chicken breasts
2 cups apple cider
½ cup mixed dried fruit, finely chopped
2 tablespoons canola oil
1½ cups vegetable stock
1½ tablespoons cornstarch
1½ tablespoons butter
flour for dredging
Salt and black pepper

Cover a cutting board with plastic wrap and lay the meat on it. Cover with another piece of plastic wrap and pound until half as thick (with chicken, try to even it out). Dredge lightly in flour. In a saucepan, heat cider and bring to a boil. Reduce heat and simmer for 10 minutes or until the cider is reduced by half. Add the fruit to cider mixture and remove from heat. In a skillet on medium high heat, heat 1 tablespoon of the oil and brown the meat for 2 to 3 minutes on each side. Work in batches and add more oil when necessary. Put on plate and cover with foil to keep warm.

In a small mixing bowl, combine the cornstarch with a little vegetable stock and whisk until smooth. Add to the skillet and whisk up the browned bits. Add the rest of the stock and the cider mixture and simmer until it starts to thicken. Add the meat back to pan and simmer 5 to 6 minutes. Add the butter and salt and pepper to taste. Drizzle the sauce over the meat and serve over rice or potatoes.

Chili Relleno Casserole

Contributed by Tanya Smart

This is a great dish to take to a potluck, as it is tasty either warm, at room temperature, or cold. The casserole makes a great breakfast, lunch, brunch, or dinner.

Serves: 4 to 6   **Prep: 20 min**   **Cooking: 45 min**

1 27-ounce can whole green chilies
3 cups cheese (cheddar, jack, Colby or
    combination), grated
5 eggs
½ cup milk
⅛ teaspoon paprika

Preheat the oven to 350°. In a 9 x 13 casserole dish, layer the chilies and cheese (with a deeper and less wide casserole, you can make 3 layers). In a mixing bowl, whisk together the milk, eggs, and paprika. Pour over the layered chilies and cheese and bake for 45 minutes, or until the top is golden and puffy.

You can layer the chilies and cheese the night before but don't add the egg mixture until just before baking or it will separate.

Cold / Hot Crab Dinner

Contributed by Sydelle Lapidus

Both of these crab recipes come from my dear friend, Michael Turrigiano, who shared his Sicilian family secrets with me.

Cold Crab Dinner

Serves: 2   **Prep: 15 min, plus 1 - 3 hrs to marinate**

    1 cooked crab, cleaned and segmented
    ¼ cup red wine vinegar
    ½ cup olive oil
    ½ bunch of parsley, chopped
    2 cloves garlic, chopped
    Black pepper

Place crab in a shallow dish. In a mixing bowl, combine the vinegar, olive oil, parsley, garlic, and black pepper to taste and mix well. Pour over the crab. Marinate 1 to 3 hours, tossing frequently. Serve with good crusty bread.

Hot Crab Dinner

Serves: 2   **Prep: 30 min**

    ⅓ cup olive oil
    2 tablespoons (¼ stick) butter
    6 cloves garlic
    1 cooked crab, cleaned and segmented
    Juice of 1 lemon
    1 lemon, thinly sliced
    ½ bunch parsley, chopped

Preheat the oven to 200°. In a skillet, heat the olive oil and butter and sauté the garlic. Add the crab and the lemon juice and cook until just warm. Lay the lemon slices on top of the crab and move pan to the oven for 10 minutes, or just enough to warm the crab as it is already cooked and can dry out. Pull from oven. Toss with parsley and serve with good bread.

Crispy Spiced Duckling

Contributed by Myra Beals

Serves: 4   **Prep: 10 min, plus overnight for marinade**   **Cooking: 2 hrs**

1 4½-pound duckling, quartered

2 medium scallions (green onions), cut in 2-inch pieces and crushed with side of knife

2 teaspoons salt

¼ teaspoon fennel seeds

1 teaspoon red pepper, crushed

¼ teaspoon ground cloves

¼ teaspoon ground ginger

1 tablespoon soy sauce

2 tablespoons honey

Rub duckling quarters with scallion pieces and discard the scallions. In a small bowl, combine the salt, red pepper, fennel seeds, cloves, and ginger and mix. Rub duckling quarters with spice mixture. In a large bowl, place duckling and cover and refrigerate overnight. Preheat the oven to 350°. On a rack in a roasting pan, roast duckling quarters skin side down for 2 hours. During last 15 minutes of roasting, brush duckling quarters with soy sauce and then honey. Serve hot.

Gabi's Chicken Casserole

Contributed by the Fienburgh Family

This has been one of our favorite recipes for 30 years. Our kids begged for the recipe when they moved into their own homes and every dinner guest that we've served this dish has loved it. It's our pleasure to share this with you.

Serves: 6 to 8   **Prep: 30 min**   **Cooking: 1½ hrs**

8 to 10 chicken thighs
3 tablespoons olive oil or butter
4 medium carrots, peeled and cut into quarter-inch rounds
1 medium onion, peeled and diced
1 medium turnip, peeled and cut into half-inch cubes
2 stalks broccoli, cut into florets
8 potatoes, halved
¼ teaspoon salt
⅛ teaspoon black pepper
1 cup Sauvignon Blanc or Chardonnay
1 14½-ounce can diced tomatoes
3 or 4 cloves garlic, pressed
1 cup heavy whipping cream

Preheat the oven to 375°. Wash chicken in cold water and dry. In a heavy roasting pan with a lid or Dutch oven on medium heat, heat the olive oil. Add the chicken and brown on both sides. Remove the chicken and let it rest for a moment. Drain off the chicken fat and leave behind about 2 tablespoons. Place the carrots evenly into the bottom of the pan. Put the chicken pieces on top of carrots and then add onion, turnip, broccoli, and potatoes. Season with salt and pepper, and add the wine. Cover and cook chicken for 1 hour. Drain and rinse the tomatoes in a sieve and add garlic. Remove pan from the oven and add the tomato mixture. Cook for another 15 minutes. Remove pan again and add the cream. Cook another 15 minutes. Chicken should be cooked through and potatoes should be soft. Serve while steaming hot. It's delicious with fresh crusty baguette or ciabatta.

Glazed Chicken

Contributed by Fred Ash

Serves: 4   **Prep: 1 hr**

Olive oil spray
4 chicken breasts, halved and boneless
½ teaspoon seasoned salt
½ teaspoon oregano
⅓ cup apricot jam
2 tablespoons honey
2 tablespoons brandy
⅓ cup water
1 tablespoon cornstarch

Preheat the oven to 375°. Spray 6 x 8 baking pan with olive oil. Place chicken in pan and sprinkle with seasoned salt and oregano. Cover and bake for 20 minutes. In a mixing bowl, combine jam, honey, and brandy and pour over chicken. Bake for 10 minutes or more uncovered. Remove chicken and set aside. Deglaze pan and pour into a saucepan. Add water and cornstarch and simmer until the sauce is thick and clear. Serve chicken with sauce over mashed potatoes.

Grandma Jung's Sauerkraut and Dumplings

Contributed by Nancy Jung

My grandmother was a terrible cook, except for this one dish that all her grand-children loved.

Serves: 4   **Prep: 1 hr**

4 pork chops
1 jar sauerkraut (32 ounces)
1 sweet apple, peeled, cored, and diced
1 tablespoon brown sugar
¼ teaspoon caraway seeds
1½ cups flour
2 teaspoons baking powder
¾ teaspoon salt
3 tablespoons butter
¾ cup milk

In a skillet, fry the pork chops until browned and the juices are seared in. In a large saucepan, place the sauerkraut along with the sauerkraut jar of water and the apple. Place the pork chops in the saucepan, a tablespoon or two of brown sugar and sprinkle with caraway seeds. Bring to a boil, lower to a simmer, and cook with the lid on for an hour.

For the dumplings: In a mixing bowl, combine the flour, baking powder, and salt and sift together. Cut in the butter using a pastry knife until the dough forms into crumbs. Stir in the milk a little at a time and roll out dough on a floured surface until thin. Cut into 1-inch by 1-inch pieces and drop into the simmering pork chops and sauerkraut. Cook for 10 minutes uncovered, and another 10 minutes with the lid on. Serve immediately. Place a few dumplings on the plate and smother with sauerkraut before adding a pork chop for each serving.

Paprika Chicken

Contributed by Sydelle Lapidus

I got this recipe from my dear mother-in-law, Blanca Dominitz, who cooked it in the former Czechoslovakia and Vienna. I think of her whenever I make it.

Serves: 6   **Prep: 50 min**

1 large chicken, cut in 12 pieces
3 large onions, sliced
2½ tablespoons paprika
Water
Salt to taste

In a heavy soup pot, place the onions in the bottom. Add the chicken pieces and sprinkle with paprika. Add a splash of water and salt. Refrain from adding more water, as the onions will provide plenty of liquid. Cover and cook on low for 25 minutes, or until chicken is cooked but not dry.

Serve over noodles or mashed potatoes. Have good bread nearby to sop up the fabulous sauce.

Roberta's Spinach Quiche

Contributed by Roberta Morrow

Serve with a green salad for a delightful light dinner.

Serves: 6 to 8   **Prep: 20 to 30 min**   **Cooking: 45 min**

1 tablespoon butter, melted
1 prepared 9-inch piecrust (I use Pillsbury)
6 large eggs
¼ cup garlic, minced
¼ cup onion, minced
¼ cup fresh parsley, chopped
Salt and pepper
1 large bag fresh spinach or 2 boxes frozen spinach, lightly steamed
1½ cups sharp cheddar cheese (or jack, hot pepper jack, or your favorite combination), shredded
Paprika

Preheat oven to 350°. Coat a 9-inch glass pie dish with butter or nonstick spray. Lay the piecrust in the dish and mold to fit the edge. In a medium-sized bowl, whip the eggs and add the garlic, onion, and parsley, and salt and pepper to taste. Drain the spinach and add to the egg mixture (there will be more spinach than egg). Pour egg and spinach mixture into the piecrust and evenly sprinkle the cheese on top. Sprinkle with paprika and bake for 45 minutes, or until a knife inserted in the center doesn't come out gooey.

June's Spinach Quiche

Contributed by June Lemos

This vegetarian quiche is a favorite of my sister, Jone. She taught me how to make it when we were both in college in the mid-1970s. Since then I've stolen it from her and made the dish my own. It was our mother TJ's favorite, and is also a big hit at alto sectionals.

Serves: 8   **Prep: 20 min**   **Cooking: 35 min**

1 sleeve (40) saltine crackers
½ cup (one stick) butter
1½ pounds spinach, fresh or 10 ounces frozen
1 bunch scallions (green onions), chopped
2 cups Swiss cheese, shredded
2 eggs
1 cup sour cream
1 teaspoon allspice
dash of white pepper
1 tablespoon paprika

Preheat the oven to 375°. Place the crackers in a plastic bag and crush with a rolling pin until uniformly ground into fine crumbs. Transfer crumbs to a 9-inch glass pie pan. Melt butter and set aside one tablespoon. Add the melted butter to the cracker crumbs and mix well. Press mixture into the pie pan to form a crust. In a medium saucepan, steam the spinach until wilted (or use thawed frozen spinach) and press out excess water. In a skillet, heat the remaining butter and sauté the green onions. Place the spinach in an even layer on top of the crust and cover with the sautéed onions. In a medium bowl, combine the cheese, eggs, sour cream, allspice, and white pepper and mix well. Pour on top of the spinach and onion mixture and make sure it is completely covered. Sprinkle paprika over the top. Bake for 35 minutes or until set. Let cool slightly before serving.

Vegan Ginger Pine-Nut Stir-Fry

Contributed by Janice Culliford

Serves: 2   **Prep: 15 min**   **Cooking: 15 min**

2 tablespoons coconut oil
4 ounces extra firm (Wildwood) tofu cut into 1-inch cubes
2 small carrots, sliced half-inch thick
1 medium burdock root or parsnip, sliced quarter-inch thick
1 small beet, sliced
½ medium onion, diced
2 teaspoons fresh ginger, minced or grated
1 head broccoli, chopped
1 cup shitake mushrooms, thinly sliced
8 Brussels sprouts
1 medium zucchini, sliced ½-inch thick
¼ cup pine nuts
3 cloves garlic
½ Meyer lemon
Bragg Liquid Aminos or soy sauce

In a large wok or skillet, heat coconut oil on medium high heat. Sauté the tofu for 3 minutes, or until it is golden brown on all sides. Add the carrots, burdock, beet, onion, and ginger and sauté for another 3 minutes. Add the broccoli, mushrooms, and Brussels sprouts and sauté for another 3 minutes. Add the zucchini, garlic, and pine nuts and mix well. Turn off the heat, put on lid, and let sit for 2 minutes. Squeeze the lemon and add Bragg Liquid Aminos to taste. Serve by itself or over rice.

Zattu's Fish Curry

Contributed by Zattu Kadan

Serves: 6   **Prep: 45 min**

2 tablespoons sunflower oil
1 large onion, cut in half and sliced
4 cloves garlic, minced
1 tablespoon fresh ginger, grated
3 cups butternut squash, cooked, peeled, and cut in 1-inch chunks
3 carrots, sliced
1 cup shitake or crimini mushrooms, sliced
2 tablespoons red curry powder
4 stalks celery, sliced
1 red bell pepper, sliced
1 medium head bok choy, sliced
1 cup water
Salt
1 14-ounce can coconut milk
1 pound red snapper or fresh local fish filets, de-boned, cut into 3-inch sections

In a wok or large skillet on medium high heat, heat the oil and sauté the onions, garlic and ginger briefly. Add the squash and carrots and sauté for 5 minutes or until almost tender. Add the mushrooms and curry powder and cook for 2 minutes. Add the celery and cook briefly. Add the bell pepper and sauté until vegetables are barely tender. Do not overcook. Add the bok choy and stir until heated. Add the water and salt to taste. Cover and let come to simmer. Add the coconut milk and mix well. Gently place the fish on top and use ladle to cover fish and vegetables with hot liquid. Cover and simmer for 5 minutes or until fish is cooked and vegetables are tender. Don't overcook fish.

Serve on a bed of cooked whole grain. I like short grain brown rice or a mixture of grains (see next page).

One of my favorite mixtures

½ cup whole wheat berries, rinsed
2 cups water
1½ cups short grain brown rice, rinsed
1 cup quinoa, rinsed

In a heavy saucepan, place the wheat berries and lightly toast on medium heat. Add the water, cover, and gently boil for 5 minutes. Add the rice, lower heat, and cover. Let simmer for approximately 30 minutes. It should still be pretty watery. When rice is ¾ done, add quinoa and more water if necessary. Cover, reduce heat, and cook for 10 minutes or until the water is absorbed.

DESSERTS

Apple-Raisin Crumble with Orange Custard Sauce

Contributed by Carla Jupiter

Serves: 8   Prep: 1 hr   Cooking: 1 hr

14 tablespoons butter at room temperature
¼ cup + 1 tablespoon brown sugar
½ cup cornstarch
¼ teaspoon ground cloves
1⅓ cups flour
⅛ teaspoon salt
6 to 7 Golden Delicious or Fuji apples, peeled, cored, and sliced
¾ cups raisins
¼ cup brown sugar
2 tablespoons orange juice
4 large yolks
¼ cup sugar
2 cups half and half
2 teaspoon orange peel, finely grated

Preheat the oven to 325°. In a mixing bowl, beat together the butter and sugar until fluffy. Add the cornstarch, cloves, flour, and salt and mix well. Add the apples, mix well, and spread in an 11 x 8 Pyrex baking dish. In another mixing bowl, combine the raisins, sugar, and orange juice, and mix well. Scatter the raisin mixture over the apple mixture and press to compact slightly. Bake for an hour or until apples are tender and crumble is golden.

For the custard: In a mixing bowl, whisk together the yolks and sugar until well mixed. In a saucepan, combine the half and half and the orange peel, and heat to simmer. Gradually whisk the half and half mixture into the yolk mixture, and pour into the saucepan. Stir while heating the custard on medium low heat for 4 minutes, or until the custard thickens slightly and the temperature is 180°. Do not boil. Refrigerate until cold, about 4 hours. Serve with crumble at room temperature. Spoon chilled custard over each serving.

Aunt Sue's Pecan Pie

Contributed by Meadow

Serves: 6   **Prep: 15 min**   **Cooking: 45 min**

3 eggs
½ cup sugar
¼ teaspoon salt
1 cup light corn syrup
½ teaspoon vanilla extract
1½ cups pecans, crushed
Pecan halves for garnish

Preheat oven to 300°. In a mixing bowl, add the eggs and beat slightly. Add the other ingredients and mix well. Prepare a piecrust (see "No-Fail Pie Crust," page 109) and pour in the filling. Bake for 45 minutes on lower rack. Cool thoroughly and cover with whipped cream, and decorate top with pecan halves in a sunflower pattern. Pie is best served at room temperature.

Variations: For a nuttier pie, add another ¼ cup of pecans and an extra egg. Use a deep-dish pie pan as it has a tendency to spill over. To substitute honey for the sugar, add an extra egg to thicken the mixture.

Bread Pudding with Whiskey Sauce

Contributed by Ledford House

Serves: 6   **Prep: 15 min**   **Cooking: 40 min**

6 cups white bread, cut into cubes
8 cups (½ gallon) milk
6 eggs
3 cups sugar
2 cups black raisins
4 tablespoons vanilla extract
1 tablespoon cinnamon
1 teaspoon nutmeg

Preheat the oven to 350°. In a large mixing bowl, combine bread and milk and let soak from one hour to overnight. Crush bread with hands to make sure milk is soaked through. In another bowl, combine the remaining ingredients and stir well. Add the bread and milk mixture and pour into a 9 x 13 baking pan. Bake for 40 minutes or until firm. Serve warm with whiskey sauce poured on individual servings with (optional) whipped cream.

Whiskey Sauce

1 cup (2 sticks) butter
2 cups powdered sugar
2 eggs, beaten
4 ounces bourbon whiskey

In a double boiler on medium high heat, cream the sugar and butter until very hot and the sugar dissolves. Whisk the eggs quickly into sugar mixture so the eggs don't curdle. Add the whiskey.

Chocolate Macadamia Tart

Contributed by Carla Jupiter

Serves: 8 to 10   **Prep: 1 hr 45 min**   **Cooking: 40 min**

½ recipe Pâte Sucrée
2 large eggs
2 cups white sugar
½ tablespoon bourbon whiskey
½ cup all purpose flour
¾ cup (1½ sticks) unsalted butter, melted and cooled
¼ teaspoon salt
6 ounces semi-sweet chocolate, coarsely chopped
2½ cups whole unsalted macadamia nuts

On a lightly floured surface, roll the Pâte Sucrée out to a 14-inch round. Press into the bottom and sides of an 11-inch tart pan, and trim along edge. Set aside in the refrigerator for 30 minutes. Preheat the oven to 400°. In a mixing bowl, whisk together the eggs, sugar, and bourbon. Whisk in the flour and salt, and then the butter. Stir in chocolate and pour into Pâte Sucrée shell. Arrange nuts on top and press gently. Bake for 10 minutes. Reduce heat to 350° and bake for 30 minutes, or until nuts and pâte sucrée are golden. Cover with foil if the tart browns too fast. Cool completely on a wire rack before serving. This tart can be stored airtight at room temperature for 2 days.

Pâte Sucrée for 2 tarts

2½ cups all purpose flour
1 cup (2 sticks) unsalted butter
3 tablespoons sugar
2 large egg yolks
¼ cup ice water

In a food processor, combine the flour and sugar and process for 10 seconds. Add the butter and process for another 10 seconds. In a mixing bowl, combine the yolks and water and lightly beat. Add the yolk mixture in a slow stream to processor for 30 seconds. Remove dough and divide into 2 pieces. Make a disc of each and wrap in plastic. Refrigerate for an hour before using.

Chocolate Orange Gelato

Contributed by Dirk Jahelka

This is a great after-choir treat.

Serves: 10   **Prep: 2 hrs**

¼ cup (½ stick) butter, melted
1 orange, zest only
8 ounces semi-sweet bakers chocolate
2 cups milk
1 cup sugar
6 egg yolks

In a saucepan on low heat, combine the butter and zest, and simmer for 15 minutes. Strain off the zest and discard. Add the chocolate, milk, and sugar, and increase the heat to medium. Stir until the chocolate is melted. In a mixing bowl, whisk the yolks and slowly stir in the chocolate mixture to bring the yolks up to temperature. Return the mixture to the saucepan and heat until thickened. Remove from heat and let cool for one hour. Transfer mixture to an ice cream machine or freezer for 30 minutes. Serve in ice cream bowls.

Company's Comin' Pumpkin Cookies

Contributed by Karin Uphoff

This recipe got its name as I only made these cookies when company showed up. It soon became a favorite for fall back-to-school care packages.

Yield: 3 dozen **Prep: 15 min** **Cooking: 15 min**

⅔ cup sunflower oil or melted butter
2 tablespoons honey
2 tablespoons maple syrup
¼ cup molasses
1 teaspoon vanilla extract
1 cup cooked fresh or canned pumpkin
2 cups whole-wheat pastry flour
⅓ cup wheat germ
1 tablespoon cinnamon
2 teaspoons baking powder
½ teaspoon baking soda
½ teaspoon nutmeg
½ teaspoon allspice
1½ cup pecans, chopped
1 cup dark chocolate chips
⅔ cup juice-sweetened dried cranberries

Preheat the oven to 350°. In a mixing bowl, cream together the oil, honey, maple syrup, molasses, and vanilla extract. Add the pumpkin and mix well. In another bowl, sift together the flour, wheat germ, cinnamon, baking powder, baking soda, nutmeg, and allspice. Combine the wet and dry ingredients and mix thoroughly. Add the pecans, chocolate chips, and cranberries, and mix well. On a greased cookie sheet, place 1 heaping tablespoon of dough for each cookie and bake for 15 minutes, or until the underside and edges of the cookies are slightly brown. Transfer on a wire rack to cool and guard carefully.

Cranberry-Pecan Bars

Contributed by Myra Beals

Yield: 36 bars **Prep: 15 min** **Baking: 1 hr**

Crust

1 cup all purpose flour
3 tablespoons sugar
⅓ cup butter
½ cup pecans, finely chopped

Preheat the oven to 350°. Place the flour and sugar in a mixing bowl and cut the butter into flour mixture until it resembles coarse crumbs. Stir in the pecans. Press the mixture into the bottom of an ungreased 13 x 9 x 2 baking pan. Bake for 15 minutes. Remove from oven and set aside. Let the oven remain hot.

Topping

1¼ cups sugar
2 tablespoons all-purpose flour
2 eggs, beaten
2 tablespoons milk
1 tablespoon orange peel, shredded
1 teaspoon vanilla
1 cup cranberries (use fresh or frozen only), chopped
½ cup pecans, finely chopped

In a mixing bowl, combine sugar and flour. Stir in eggs, milk, orange peel and vanilla and mix well. Fold in cranberries and remaining pecans, and spread over partially baked crust. Bake for 25 to 30 minutes or until top is golden. Cool in the pan on wire rack and cut into bars while warm. Cool completely before serving.

Decadent Raw Chocolate Cake

Contributed by Lisa Norman

Lisa is a graduate of the Living Light Culinary Arts Institute, Fort Bragg, California, and attended Le Cordon Bleu, Paris, for Boulangerie. This cake is very rich. A little goes a long way.

Serves: 8 to 12   **Prep: 35 min, plus refrigerate overnight**

2 cups walnuts, soaked for 2 hours and drained
12 pitted dates
6 tablespoons cocoa or carob powder
1 teaspoon vanilla extract
1 apple, peeled and cored
6 tablespoons coconut, shredded
½ cup cashews, soaked for 2 hours and drained
¼ cup water

In a food processor with an **S**-blade, place the walnuts and process to a fine meal. Add 8 dates and process to blend. Add the cocoa powder and vanilla extract, and process to blend. Mince half of the apple and puree the other half. Add both to the walnut mixture and process to blend. In an 8-inch spring form pan, sprinkle 2 tablespoons of the coconut. Add half of the chocolate mixture and spread evenly over coconut. In a blender, combine the cashews, remaining dates, and water, and process to a thick cream. Layer half the cream on the first chocolate layer. Sprinkle 2 tablespoons of the coconut on top. Spread the remaining half of the chocolate mixture, the remaining cream, and top with the last of the coconut. Refrigerate overnight. Cut and serve chilled.

Fruit Cobbler

Contributed by Carolyn Carleton

This recipe is from my mother-in-law, Anna Carleton, in her Alabama home. Any fresh or frozen fruit can be used in this simple dessert that looks more elegant than could be guessed from the easy preparation. It is especially good with berries, peaches, and mangos.

Serves: 12　　　　　　　　　　**Prep: 20 min**　　　　　　　　　　**Cooking: 1 hr**

- 1½ cup flour
- 1½ cup sugar
- 3 teaspoons baking powder
- 1⅛ cup milk
- ½ cup (1 stick) butter, melted
- 3 cups chopped fruit, fresh or frozen

Preheat the oven to 350°. In a mixing bowl, combine the flour, sugar, and baking powder. Mix well and add the milk, and blend until smooth. In 13 x 9 x 2 glass baking dish, pour the butter. Pour batter over the butter and drop fruit over all. Do not stir. Bake for an hour or until browned. Serve hot with ice cream.

Janny's Cardamom Delights

Contributed by Janice Culliford

Yield: 12 cookies　　　　　**Prep: 15 min**　　　　　**Cooking: 15 min**

½ cup sugar
½ cup margarine
½ teaspoon vanilla extract
1 tablespoon water
1½ cups wheat flour (rice or gluten free flour)
1½ teaspoons ground cardamom
¼ teaspoon baking soda
12 walnut pieces (*optional*)
½ cup confectionary sugar

Preheat the oven to 350°. In mixing bowl, combine the sugar and margarine and stir until smooth. Add the vanilla and water and stir until smooth. In another mixing bowl, combine the flour, 1 teaspoon of the cardamom, and baking soda, and mix well. Gradually add the dry ingredients to the wet ingredients until completely mixed. Form 1-inch balls and flatten them with the bottom of a juice glass. Place on a slightly greased cookie sheet about 1 inch apart and press 1 walnut piece in the center of each cookie. Bake for about 12 to 15 minutes.

In small mixing bowl, combine the confectionary sugar and remaining cardamom, and mix well. Take slightly cooled cookies and roll each side in the mix. Put on plate and serve.

Low-Calorie Berry Pie

Contributed by Agnes Woolsey

Serves: 8   Prep: 40 min   Cooking: 40 min

4 cups blueberries or blackberries, rinsed and drained
¼ cup tapioca pearls
½ cup water
1 teaspoon powdered Stevia
6 or 8 sticks of rhubarb, cut in one half-inch chunks
2 frozen prepared piecrusts
¼ cup coconut flour
¼ cup (½ stick) butter, cold
1 lemon, juice only

Preheat the oven to 400°. In a large mixing bowl, combine the berries, tapioca, and water, and sprinkle with the Stevia (1 teaspoon of Stevia is equal to 1 cup of sugar). Add the rhubarb and let soak for 15 minutes so that the tapioca will swell with liquid from berries and rhubarb.

Place 1 piecrust in a 9-inch glass baking-dish and fill with the berry mixture. Let the other piecrust warm to room temperature. Sprinkle coconut flour and lemon juice on top of the berry mixture. Add dabs of the butter, and use wet fingers to dampen the rim of the lower piecrust so it is sticky. Set the second piecrust over the filled piecrust and match the edges. Press the edges together with a fork and make fluting edges by pressing 2 fingers on the crust and lifting the dough between the fingers so it looks like ocean waves. Bake for 40 minutes or when crust is golden brown. Allow pie to cool and set for half an hour before serving.

Mom's Famous Sour Cream Coffee Cake

Contributed by Myra Beals

Serves: 8   **Prep: 15 min**   **Cooking: 45 min**

1 cup sugar
½ cup (1 stick) butter
2 cups flour
1 teaspoon baking powder
1 teaspoon baking soda
2 eggs
1 teaspoon vanilla extract
½ pint sour cream
½ cup pecans, chopped
½ cup sugar
2 tablespoons cinnamon

Preheat oven to 350°. In a large mixing bowl, cream the sugar and butter. In another bowl, combine the flour, baking powder, and baking soda and mix well. Add the eggs one at a time to the butter mixture and blend well after each egg. Add the vanilla and mix well. Add the flour mixture alternately with sour cream and mix well. In another bowl, combine the pecans, sugar, and cinnamon and set aside. In a 9 x 13 x 2 pan, pour half the batter and sprinkle with half of the pecan mixture. Add the rest of the batter and sprinkle the rest of the topping. Bake for 45 minutes or until golden brown.

Nana's Texas Lemon Meringue Pie

Contributed by Alex Pierangeli

This big, simple, and decadent pie was a tradition in our house when I was a little girl. My daddy made it at least once a month from his mother's recipe. It was my favorite dessert in a house of dessert eaters and dessert makers. I now make it only for very special occasions; you'll see why.

Living on the Coast, it's hard to achieve the height of meringues we used to have in West Texas where the humidity commonly hovered around 3 to 5 per cent. There's nothing like the tang of the lemon contrasted with the richness of the filling and the fluffy topping, and the crust only gets better as the pie ages a day or two (if you can keep it around that long).

Serves: 6 to 8　　　　　　　　　**Prep: 30 min**　　　　　　　　　**Baking: 30 min**

Graham Cracker Crust

　　1⅔ packages of graham crackers (packages come 3 to a box)
　　½ cup (1 stick), melted
　　¼ to ½ cup of sugar

Preheat the oven to 425°. Put the graham crackers in a clean bag with lots of room left over. Use a rolling pin to crush the crackers to a coarse, but even consistency. In a mixing bowl, combine the crushed crackers, butter, and sugar. (You can leave out the sugar, but it makes for a smoother crust, even just 1 tablespoon.) Mix well with a fork until the ingredients are well blended. Pour the mixture into a deep, 9-inch tart pan. With your fingers, press the mixture evenly on the bottom and around the sides of the pan to a thickness of ¼ inch. Place crust in oven and bake for 10 to 15 minutes or until crust starts to brown. Remove and set aside. Lower the oven temperature to 350°.

Lemon Filling

　　5 lemons
　　5 egg yolks
　　1⅔ 14-ounce cans of sweetened condensed milk

Juice the lemons and strain the juice to remove seeds and most of the pulp. In a mixing bowl, combine the lemon juice, egg yolks, and sweetened condensed milk. Whisk or use an electric mixer on medium, beating until the filling thickens a bit. Pour into baked crust.

Meringue

5 egg whites, room temperature
¼ teaspoon cream of tartar
6 tablespoons (⅜ of a cup) white sugar

All utensils for making the meringue must be clean and grease-free. In a deep metal or ceramic bowl, place the egg whites. Use an electric mixer on low to beat the whites until they are foamy. Add the cream of tartar and continue to beat. As the meringue thickens, increase the mixer speed from low to medium. When the meringue is fluffy with a fine texture, add the sugar a little at a time while you continue to mix. Continue beating until the sugar is well blended and the meringue forms stiff peaks. Carefully scoop the meringue on top of the pie filling and spread around the edges. Make peaks by pressing lightly on the meringue with a knife and lifting off quickly. Place the pie in the middle of the oven rack and cook at 350° for 10 to 15 minutes or until the peaks are brown and the entire meringue is golden brown. Remove and let cool on a wire rack before serving.

The pie can be refrigerated overnight and served cold, but the meringue will droop a bit from the moisture. This does not affect the flavor.

Variation: You can make smaller, shallower pie with one can of sweetened condensed milk, 3 eggs, 3 lemons and a package plus a couple of graham crackers. You can even use low-fat sweetened condensed milk.

No-Fail Pie Crusts

Contributed by Meadow

These crusts might seem dry as you roll them out, but they do make wonderful, flaky crusts.

Yield: 2 crusts   **Prep: 15 min**

Pie Crust #1

3 cups flour
2 teaspoons salt
1½ cups shortening
1 egg
5 tablespoons water
1 teaspoon vinegar

In a mixing bowl, combine the flour and salt, and mix well. Cut in the shortening with a pastry knife or use a food processor. In another bowl, beat the egg with water and vinegar. Add to the flour mixture and mix well. Roll out the piecrust on a lightly floured surface.

If you only need one crust, just cut the recipe in half.

Pie Crust #2

1¼ cups shortening
3 cups flour
1 teaspoon salt
1 egg
5 tablespoons water
1 tablespoon vinegar

In a mixing bowl, cut the shortening into flour and salt. In another bowl, combine the egg, water, and vinegar. Pour liquid into flour mixture and blend with spoon until flour is moistened. Roll out the piecrust on a lightly floured board. This is easy to handle and can be re-rolled without toughening.

Rollo's Cheesecake

Contributed by Rollo Dilworth
(Rollo is the choir director and composer who inspired our trip to London in 2012.)

I made this cheesecake every New Year's Day when I lived in Chicago. It became so popular that I had to start baking two of them.

Serves: 12   **Prep: 15 min**   **Cooking: 45 min**

3 8-ounce packages of Philadelphia cream cheese
5 eggs
1¼ cups sugar
1 tablespoon vanilla extract
1 can (8 ounces) Pillsbury Refrigerated Crescent Dinner Rolls

Preheat the oven to 325°. Allow cream cheese to reach room temperature and become quite soft. In a large mixing bowl, place the soft cream cheese and gradually mix in the eggs and sugar. Add the vanilla extract. The mixture should be similar to cake batter. Open the crescent rolls and allow the dough to unroll into one complete sheet. In a glass 9 x 13 x 2 baking dish, place the dough and use your fingers to flatten the sheet so that it completely covers the bottom. Pour the batter into the baking dish and place in the center of the oven to bake for 45 minutes, or until the edges are golden brown. Let cool and chill in refrigerator overnight before serving.

Sally's Heavenly Dairy-Free Whipped Cream

Contributed by Sally Fletcher

Serves: 4 to 6   **Prep: Overnight in refrigerator, then 15 min**

1 14-ounce can coconut milk
½ cup powdered sugar
¼ teaspoon vanilla extract
Pinch of cinnamon

Place the coconut milk in the refrigerator overnight.

Place the mixer bowl and the whisk into the freezer for 3 hours to chill. Open the coconut milk at the bottom with a bottle opener to drain off the coconut water, and discard the water. Open the top of the can and scoop out the thick cream, and place in bowl. Add the vanilla extract and cinnamon. Start the mixer on low and move up 1 or 2 notches until you get to moderate speed. As it starts to whip, gradually add in the sugar. Once the mixture looks fluffy like fresh whipped cream, it's ready. Any extra keeps well in the fridge.

Sweetheart Truffles

Contributed by Tanya Smart

Yield: 24 truffles **Prep: 20 min** **Chill: 3 hrs**

6 ounces dark chocolate chips (or bar, finely chopped)
⅓ cup heavy cream
2 tablespoons butter, room temperature

Finishing touches
½ cup cocoa powder
½ cup sprinkles
½ cup turbinado or raw sugar
½ cup chocolate, melted

In a mixing bowl, place the chocolate chips. In a saucepan, place cream and heat to barely boiling (steaming), and pour over the chocolate chips. Wait 1 minute and then whisk the mixture until the chocolate chips are melted and the mixture is smooth and shiny. Whisk in the butter until completely mixed. Cover and refrigerate for 3 hours or until firm. Scoop out teaspoonfuls of the mixture and roll between your palms to form cherry-sized balls. Roll in the finishing touches as desired. Cover and refrigerate until serving. You can also hand out spoons and let guests do their own.

MISCELLANEOUS

Dog Cookies: Peanut Butter and Banana Biscotti

Contributed by Tanya Smart

Canines will seek you out and raid your pockets for these biscotti.

Yield: 5 dozen　　　　　　　**Prep: 30 min**　　　　　　　**Baking: 50 min**

5 cups whole-wheat flour
1 cup wheat germ
1 egg
2 medium bananas, over-ripe, frozen, and thawed
⅓ cup peanut butter
1 cup water

Preheat the oven to 350°. In a mixer with a dough hook, combine all ingredients and mix until dough is stiff but workable. On a lightly floured surface, roll the dough out to a 1½ inch wide log and slice biscotti style. Place on an ungreased baking sheet and bake for 50 minutes, or until firm to the touch but not burned. Turn off the heat and allow the biscotti to cool in the oven until hard. Store in a sealed container. They last a long time when dried and hardened properly.

Index

Index